Nifast
Care of the Older Person

Care of the Older Person
FETAC Level 5

Nifast

Gill & Macmillan

Gill & Macmillan
Hume Avenue
Park West
Dublin 12
www.gillmacmillan.ie

© Nifast 2013

978 07171 5725 9

Print origination by Síofra Murphy
All images courtesy of Shutterstock and Presenter Media
Printed by GraphyCems, Spain

Contents

Chapter 1 Ageing Process

Chapter outline 2

Defining healthy ageing 2

    How we grow old 3

    Why we grow old 4

Global and national demographic trends 5

    Diminishing labour force 8

    The ageing population 9

    Incidence of disease 10

    Geographical variation 10

Physical diseases that can occur in the older person 11

    Normal signs of ageing 11

    Urinary signs of ageing 12

    Other signs of ageing 12

    Physical diseases when ageing 13

Physiological process of ageing 15

Psychological process of ageing 16

Social impact of ageing 17

Differing attitudes to ageing 18

Healthcare assistant's role in promoting positive attitudes to ageing .. 19

Statutory and voluntary agencies in promoting wellbeing 21

    Statutory agencies 21

    Voluntary and independent provision 22

    Private providers 23

Understanding the concept and practice of preparation for
   retirement 23
Ethnic and cultural influences on the older person 25
Useful terms and definitions 29
Revision questions 36

Chapter 2 Working with the Older Person

Chapter outline 38
Needs of the older person 38
   Social needs 40
   Emotional needs 40
   Psychological needs 41
   Recreational needs 42
   Financial needs 43
   Environmental needs 43
   Spiritual needs 44
      How can spiritual needs be met? 45
Role of the healthcare assistant 45
Communicating effectively 47
Empowerment 49
Advocacy 50
Independence 51
Individualised care 51
   The 12 Activities of Daily Living 52
Dignity 52
Choice 53
   Constraints on choice 54
   Ways to facilitate choice 54

Respect 55

Self-esteem 55

Including family/carers as partners in care 55

Personal effectiveness in the workplace 56

Health promotion for older clients 58

Therapeutic interventions 64

Revision questions 66

Chapter 3 Caring for Older People with Specific Needs

Chapter outline 68

Identifying and adapting care and practices 68

Cognitive impairment and the older person 69

Sensory impairment and the older person 71

Mental illness and the older person 72

    Stigma 76

    Dementia 77

Conditions requiring immediate attention 79

Impact of living with chronic illness 85

    Impact on family and main carers 86

Elder abuse 86

    Demographic characteristics of people who reported

    mistreatment 87

Common conditions in the older person 88

    Chronic obstructive airways disease 88

    Stroke 88

    Arthritis 91

        Osteoarthritis 91

        Rheumatoid arthritis 92

Individual needs of the dying older person and their family 93

    Aspects of nursing care 96

    Dealing with fear in the dying older person and their family 96

    Dying Person's Bill of Rights 97

Respectfully carrying out duties after death 98

    Duties after death 99

Revision questions 101

Chapter 4 Care Settings

Chapter outline 103

Care settings for the older person 103

    Members of the healthcare team in each care setting 105

        General hospitals 105

        Residential homes 105

        Psychiatric hospitals 105

        Nursing homes/residential facilities 106

        Community day centres 106

        Home settings 107

        Retirement villages 107

        Hospices 107

    Support for the older person 107

    Available social services for the older person 108

        Education 108

        Retirement/leaving the workplace 109

        Leisure 111

Quality assurance 113

    Standards 113

    Quality 113

Quality of life 114

Quality of care 114

Health Information and Quality Authority 115

Revision questions 120

Abbreviations used in healthcare 121

Terminology used in nursing 121

Guide to falls prevention in the home 125

Glossary 127

Course information 132

References 133

Chapter 1

Ageing Process

Chapter Outline

- Defining healthy ageing.

- Global and national demographic trends.

- Physical diseases that can occur in the older person.

- Physiological process of ageing.

- Psychological process of ageing.

- Social impact of ageing.

- Differing attitudes to ageing.

- Healthcare assistant's role in promoting positive attitudes to ageing.

- Statutory and voluntary agencies in promoting wellbeing.

- Understanding the concept and practice of preparation for retirement.

- Ethnic and cultural influences on the older person.

Defining Healthy Ageing

Normal ageing refers to the time-related processes that affect everyone as they grow older. The process of ageing is very gradual and natural, and it is hardly noticeable to us. Each individual will age in different ways depending on a number of factors.

Where we live in the world is a factor: people in the west live longer than those in the third world. (Consider the reasons for this.) Ageing can be affected by our environment: whether we are rich or poor, the position in society we hold, the type of job we do and housing we live in. Our lifestyle can affect the ageing process: what we eat and drink and abuses of the same, the amount of exercise we take, drug abuse, smoking and sexual habits.

Social factors have an affect also, such as outlook on life, good relationships with family and friends, and a strong support system in our community. Inherited or genetic factors such as diseases or traits, and whether we are male or female (females have a longer lifespan) contribute. All of the above factors will have an effect on the normal process of ageing.

How We Grow Old

There are many theories of how and why we age. Those theories are still largely unproven. One such theory leads us to believe that the body is pre-programmed with a lifespan. Other theories suggest that cell replacement cannot keep pace with cell death, and the cell replacement process simply wears out. However, we do know that the metabolic rate slows down and body cells become less efficient, which affects the functioning of the body's major organs. Our muscles, joints and ligaments become less supple, resulting in stiffness, and loss of abilities and agility.

Most elderly people complain of some degree of arthritis. As the lubricant (synovial fluid) around the joints dries up, the cartilage becomes rough and flaky, causing both friction within the joints themselves and pain. The bones/joints become enlarged and swollen, often appearing misshapen or deformed.

Osteoarthritis is a degenerative disease, which is caused mainly by 'wear and tear' of the joints. Wear and tear occurs with day-to-day activity during the lifetime of a human being. This explains why it is common in older adults. Apparently, three times more women than men are affected by the disease, which may be due to women's longer lifespans or possibly because women do more physical work.

The lens of the eye is affected by loss of elasticity and reduced focusing power results in long-sightedness. The expiratory recoil in the lungs is also affected by loss of elasticity, which can affect breathing ability and overall fitness. Body temperature becomes difficult to maintain because of an inability to move around as much or a lack of income to afford adequate home heating. This can result in hypothermia, which can frequently have fatal consequences for older adults, particularly in the winter months.

Why We Grow Old

There are also many theories as to why we grow old. There is the 'biological clock' theory, which implies that ageing results from a definite timed programme. Our lifestyle can help to speed up or slow down the biological process but, mainly, it is predetermined for us. The 'auto-immune theory' (in animals) is due to a deterioration of the immune system. This eventually results in system failure, when the body finds it difficult to differentiate foreign 'invasions' of cells (bacteria etc.) from its own cells, causing tissue breakdown and, inevitably, death.

Nutritional balance problems occur when we eat more than we need to and there is insufficient exercise. The theory is that if high energy foods are restricted but otherwise a healthy diet is maintained, lifespan can be increased (animal experiments show up to 50 per cent lifespan increase).

Global and National Demographic Trends

Demography means the study of the characteristics of a human population. These characteristics include size, growth, density, distribution etc. Longevity refers to the number of years an individual actually lives while life expectancy refers to demographic projections regarding the length of life.

Life expectancy has increased over the past number of years. Reasons for this increase include improved healthcare and medicine. For example, vaccinations, antibiotics and heart disease medication have eradicated some types of diseases. Improved social conditions, such as housing, are also a factor.

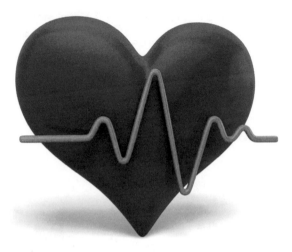

Heart disease and cancer are two of the major killers in Eire, the United Kingdom and the United States of America. Health promotion trends/ campaigns geared towards improving the life cycle of those affected, and those likely to be affected, are increasingly being stepped up. People live longer with these diseases than they used to, but they still require intensive treatment and lifestyle changes in order to survive them.

TASK

Consider current campaigns aimed at prolonging life for people with heart disease, cancer etc.

Demographic changes affect a society's healthcare and social care needs. An increase in the number of older adults in society requires an increase in both healthcare and social resources so that these needs can be met.

The healthcare resources needed include more hospital beds, nursing home beds, day hospitals, staff (to operate these additional wards) and homecare packages so that the older adult can remain at home for longer.

The social resources needed include more day centres and social outlets for older adults, including an improvement in transport to ensure that access to these events and activities are manageable for the older adult. More community resources include Meals on Wheels.

TASK

Consider other resources that the older adult may benefit from.

When government formulate policies, they should consider not just the actual demographics of a population but projected dimorphic (differences between males and females) changes also. This would enable them to plan for the future and deal effectively with situations before they arise.

TASK

Discuss the role of the Irish government.

Consider the current health service. What will it be like in 20 years when our middle-aged population have become elderly and our elderly population have become the old-old population of society?

Use the diagram on the following page to consider your answer.

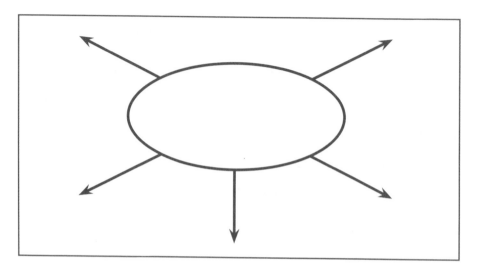

Diminishing Labour Force

The number of people available for work compared with the number of people required for jobs has a major influence on welfare policy. Predictions show that there will be a shortage of skilled and educated workers in the future. This is already evident if we consider immigration and the number of low-skilled non-national employees in Ireland. So, the number of people requiring state benefits, such as the pension, is increasing rapidly, but is the tax-paying workforce? Will the low number of children being born to families be able to fund state pensions in years to come? Could this be the reason why maternity packages are being made more attractive to women? It is also quite common to see organisations offering retirement packages nowadays.

Factors that influence population size include the following:

- Birth rate
- Death rate
- War and migration
- Emigration and immigration
- Industrialisation (caused a population increase – up to the nineteenth century, the birth and death rates had more or less balanced)

- People began to limit the number of children per family in the early part of the nineteenth century
- Medical advances
- Average of 1.8 births per woman based on age 18+ years old (below government replacement rate)
- Reduction may continue as more women pursue careers (research shows that higher earnings for women depress the birth rate; higher earnings for men increase it).

The Ageing Population

Life expectancy greatly increased in the twentieth century and the number of elderly people will continue to grow in the foreseeable future. One-fifth of the total population will be 65 and over by 2030 and 1:20 people will be dependent on some level of support from the following services:

- Statutory services
- Voluntary services
- Private services
- Family/friends.

The growing need for healthcare and social care services will prove problematic. People over 75 are heavy users of care services. Pensions and healthcare for older people will soon become the largest single budget expense. (International Labour Organization 1995)

TASK

In 1961 there were approximately six people working for every person over 65. The ratio is projected to fall to 2:8 by 2033. Consider the consequences of this.

Incidence of Disease

The decline in infectious diseases, such as measles, poliomyelitis and typhoid, has been offset by degenerative diseases, such as cancer, stroke and heart disease, caused mostly by modern lifestyle/environment, for example smoking, alcohol abuse, drug abuse, poor diet, stress and lack of exercise. However, some infectious diseases are on the increase, such as TB, hepatitis and meningitis. The incidence of food poisoning quadrupled in the 1980s.

Geographical Variation

Infant mortality rates are lower in England than in Scotland and Northern Ireland, and general health trends are better in the north than the south of England. The *Black Report* (1980) outlines the following causes of ill health:

- Physical environment
- Social and economic influence (income, wealth etc.)
- Levels of employment
- Behavioural factors – barriers to adopting a healthier lifestyle
- Access to appropriate and effective health and social services.

Healthcare varies from region to region. There is better healthcare provision in large cities such as Dublin and Galway. This gives people living in those areas the advantage of easier access to services. There are longer waiting lists for those who live in the country and have to access services in the cities, and for those who cannot afford private healthcare, such as Laya, Aviva and VHI. Accessing transport to healthcare services can also be difficult for older people as it can be costly and, indeed, uncomfortable for those with health problems. For example, consider a cancer patient travelling frequently to Dublin by train for chemotherapy.

Physical Diseases that Can Occur in the Older Person

Normal Signs of Ageing

- Nervous system changes
- Hair thins/baldness – a hereditary factor
- Loss of pigmentation – hair goes grey
- Poor eyesight – long-sightedness in the eyes
- Poor hearing – hearing declines, balance also affected
- Gum disease
- Reduced size of gums – dentures may not fit
- Sense of smell and taste affected
- Dry skin and wrinkling of skin – thinning of fat layer/loss of elasticity
- Skin fragility – increased incidence of skin tears and ulcers
- Heart shrinks/fat increases
- Metabolic rate slows
- Respiratory system less efficient
- Gallbladder less effective
- Constipation – due to lax muscle tone in bowel and lack of mobility
- Loss of calcium – shrinking of bone mass
- Less sensation in touch
- Extreme sensations of heat/cold/pain
- Muscle tone loss
- Reproductive system – hormonal changes occur

Urinary Signs of Ageing

- Urinary system less efficient – kidneys shrink, poor waste filtering
- Loss of bladder control
- Increased incidence of urinary tract infection

Other Signs of Ageing

- Ingrowing toenails
- Poor circulation
- Corns/bunions
- Ulcers
- Varicose veins
- Decrease in strength and stamina
- Deterioration in bone/muscle mass results in stooping posture

Physical Diseases when Ageing

Eyes: Cataracts

              Glaucoma

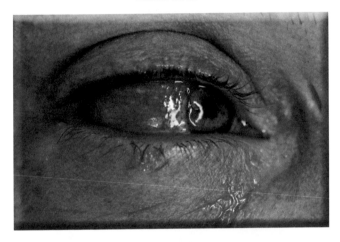

Mouth: Oral health declines

              Gum disease

              Loss of teeth

Skin: Skin irritations more common

              Warts/moles

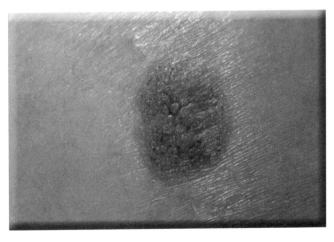

Ulcerations (quite common and
difficult to heal)
Varicose veins
Shingles

Bones and joints: Arthritis (osteoarthritis, rheumatoid)

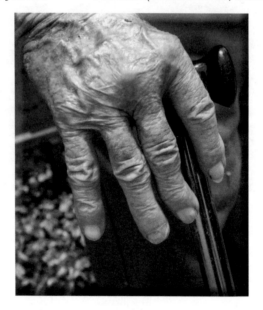

Osteoporosis (bone density decreases)

Nervous system: Hypothermia
Multiple sclerosis
Parkinson's disease

**Dementia
(acute/chronic types):**   Alzheimer's disease (most common)
Multi-infarct dementia
Pick's disease
Lewy (body dementia)

Depression: Various forms

Physiological Process of Ageing

Hair loss: The hair thins and falls out. Loss of pigmentation turns hair grey. It becomes dry and loses its natural oils, therefore becoming thin and brittle.

Muscle mass: The muscles become wasted (atrophy), causing shrinkage of muscle mass. Co-ordination and balance are affected. Wastage/shrinkage causes the older person to become less agile and tired more easily. It can also result in loss of height as posture becomes stooped.

Bones: Loss of calcium causes bones to become brittle, which can lead to frequent fractures. Hormonal changes in women can also accelerate the problem and cause osteoporosis. This can result in loss of height as posture becomes stooped.

The digestive system: The digestive system becomes less efficient, which means that food takes longer to be processed. Muscles in the gut become less effective, resulting in constipation. The kidneys are less efficient because there is kidney shrinkage, due to the fact that the pumping action of the heart has been reduced, causing less blood to go to the kidneys. The normal function of the kidneys is to filter the blood of waste products. When this is not done effectively, it causes a build-up of waste products and renders other organs less efficient.

Heart: The heart loses its efficiency. As the pumping action of the heart becomes slower, less blood is pumped to all the major organs, resulting in circulatory problems.

Lungs: The lungs lose their elasticity. Less air is inhaled, resulting in breathlessness and an inability to properly take oxygen from the air. This results in less energy.

Reproductive organs: The menopause in women results in the end of the reproductive phase of life. There is loss of vaginal lubrication and elasticity, loss of pubic hair, and the breasts shrink and drop. A man's ability to reproduce also deteriorates, although men can still father children. Sperm count is drastically reduced as is an ability to maintain an erection.

Temperature control: Temperature changes are difficult to adjust to. Hypothermia is more common.

Senses: The senses are less acute. Taste, smell and touch are affected.

Eyes and ears: Eyesight and hearing problems become more common.

Skin: The skins changes, becoming dry and pigmented. Loss of elasticity results in the skin becoming wrinkled, dry, and prone to tears and ulcers.

Psychological Process of Ageing

The psychological process of ageing refers to a deterioration in mental faculties (which is gradual). Acceptable changes can occur, which may include the older person taking longer to accept/absorb new information as intellectual processes gradually slow down. Short-term memory loss usually occurs first i.e. memory for events in the recent past are lost but those in the long-term memory can still be recalled with great clarity.

The older person can become more difficult and inflexible. They prefer to stay in familiar surroundings and tend to want their environment unchanged. It is important to remember that psychological signs of deterioration can be accelerated by a number of factors, such as loss of a partner, change of environment, older children leaving home, anxiety, depression, pain or disability which is not properly addressed.

Behavioural problems may also be a result of deterioration in an older person's condition. These can include anxiety, depression, lack of response to stimulation and low expectation.

Social Impact of Ageing

The process of growing old very often results in a number of social changes, such as retirement, bereavement and isolation, which can have a dramatic effect on the older person. The older person may long for retirement but when it eventually comes they may find that it is nothing like they had envisaged, even with the best preparation.

Retirement can bring on a sense of rejection by a society that holds no value for old people; a sense of no longer being a useful member of society. Retirement can result in a loss of status. The older person may have held down an important work position and felt that they were a valuable and useful member of a team. The loss of earning and income, as a salary is replaced by a pension, can result in a loss of self-respect.

There is extra leisure time but in some cases a lack of hobbies, interests or direction. Working life is a social life of sorts for many people, and as work colleagues are left behind so too are people who were special friends. Work colleagues/friends may not have retired yet and the older person may not want to follow any pursuits alone.

Retirement can also bring about financial problems for the older person. If no pension provision is made, it makes life very difficult; unless, of course, the older person has savings. As a result, standard of living/social lifestyle can be affected – there may be lots of free time but no money to follow any useful social hobbies or to go on outings.

Bereavement due to the loss of a partner is one of the major causes of temporary confusion in the older person. The loss of friends and work colleagues may cause the older person to face up to the inevitability of their own death, causing them to wonder when their time will come. This can cause a feeling of anxiety or depression.

A feeling of isolation develops as the older person, who does not want to be dependent, becomes increasingly dependent on family/professionals, which can cause a loss of self-respect. They may not want to ask for help, for example they may be unable to drive and live miles away from family/friends/colleagues.

Major life changes can make increasing demands, such as older children leaving home or the extra demands of becoming grandparents. Becoming a grandparent may mean that they feel obliged to help with children, a task that many old people find exhausting.

All of the factors discussed above can lead to a sense of isolation, loneliness, confusion, anxiety, depression and grief.

Differing Attitudes to Ageing

The way a society regards its ageing population is usually reflected in the way its social policy provides for its older population. The number of people living past the retirement age is constantly increasing. Since people are living longer, a great demand is being placed on the care delivery and medical services, which are in difficulty at this present time, and there will be even further strain in the coming years.

We need to look at probable changes in the pattern of the older population to see what types of needs they will have in the future. The following needs should be considered:

- Physical
- Psychological
- Medical
- Social
- Emotional.

TASK

Who will be responsible for the provision of services?

Look at local, national, voluntary and statutory services. How can we change/improve society's attitude to the older person?

What is the role of the healthcare assistant?

We also ought to give people of pre-retirement age the opportunity to 'prepare for old age' by going on pre-retirement courses: 'forewarned is forearmed'.

TASK

Consider what other roles the older person could fulfil in society. Write a list of these potential roles.

Healthcare Assistant's Role in Promoting Positive Attitudes to Ageing

From a health promotion point of view, people should start to prepare early on in life for the changes that are likely to occur in old age. There are certain things that can be done to promote health in the older person and to help them live to a healthy old age. Physical and mental deterioration cannot be altered but it can be slowed down.

It is important to nurture a healthy and positive attitude to life. People who adopt a positive attitude learn how to turn negative situations to their advantage. They tend to utilise their mental as well as physical faculties better and are, in general, happier people. Happy people laugh more. Laughter is healing and when people laugh properly and heartily endorphins are released in the brain which create a 'feel-good factor'.

The same principle applies to choosing friends. Happy people choose friends who have similar attitudes or outlooks to themselves. It is important that friendships are nurtured, too. Friends are invaluable; they act as counsellors, good company and are there to help when there are problems to be dealt with. Therefore, a healthy social life is vital.

Hobbies and interests should be within physical capabilities. They can help to boost confidence, increase muscle tone and stretch psychological capacity.

As healthcare professionals, we have a role to play in promoting positive attitudes to older adults. We can do this in our day-to-day lives by showing respect for our elders by giving up seats on the bus, holding doors open etc. We can also ensure to promote positive attitudes towards older adults by not engaging in ageist conversations, advocating their needs when necessary and speaking positively about the job we do.

Statutory and Voluntary Agencies in Promoting Wellbeing

Statutory agencies are those that are provided by law and funded by the government. The government department that is responsible for the health of the nation is the Department of Health. Heading the department is the minister for health and a support minister, who helps to run the department.

Voluntary agencies are independent agencies that provide services by contract which has to be tendered for. Voluntary agencies can also be provided by charitable agencies and public funding.

Statutory Agencies

- GPs
- Community nursing services
- Local authority departments
- Dentists
- Physiotherapists

- Chemists
- Chiropodists
- Opticians
- Orthodontists
- Ambulance services
- Paramedics
- Hospitals
- Residential care
- Health Service Executive

Voluntary and Independent Provision

- Local support groups

- Residential care
- Age Concern
- Community services centres
- Charity shops
- Home care

- Red Cross

- Meals on Wheels

- Helplines (usually non-profit making)

Private agencies are those that are funded by service users or through private health insurance such as VHI, Aviva Health etc.

Private Providers

- Private hospitals

- Orthodontists

- Physiotherapists

- Chiropodists

Understanding the Concept and Practice of Preparation for Retirement

People spend between 10 and 15 years of their lives in retirement. During midlife adults should start preparing physically, psychologically and financially for retirement. Being prepared is the best way to make a retirement enjoyable. Pre-retirement counselling and courses are widely available.

In retirement there is a considerable increase of free time. Older adults may need to be educated on how to make the best use of their leisure time; they may even need to learn how to develop leisure pursuits. The leisure choices need to be suitable for age and body function; they also need to be fulfilling and stimulating. There may be a fall in income if adequate provision for pension has not been made; therefore, leisure activities should be aimed at older people of all income/financial brackets.

On the whole, women tend to enjoy socio-cultural and home-centred activities while men enjoy outdoor activities, such as hunting, fishing and sports (playing and observing). Below is a list of the most common leisure activities chosen by older people:

- Reading
- Writing
- Television
- Arts and crafts

- Games
- Walking
- Visiting family/friends
- Physical activities
- Gardening
- Travel/camping
- Club/organisation activities
- Outings with other retired members
- Dancing.

In the early part of the century, most people did not have a choice between working and retirement. Social security provision and private pension plans have allowed people to retire earlier. Initially social security was meant to supplement a worker's personal savings and investments for retirement but has now become, in over 90 per cent of cases, their only means of support. (Parnes *et al.* 1986)

Overall, the older people who adjust best to retirement usually have made adequate provision for income; they are fit and active, and generally well educated; they have a good social network which includes family and friends; and they were usually quite satisfied with their lives before they retired. (Palmore *et al.* 1985) If older people have not made provision for retirement, and suffer from medical problems and family problems, which occur in or around retirement, then they find retirement difficult and stressful.

Women tend to be more vulnerable than men. However, if they are well balanced and well educated, and have made good investment/monetary provision, they are more likely to cope better. Nonetheless, some women may find they have great difficulty in disengaging from their working life (especially if they held a responsible work position).

This may result in a loss of self-image, sense of usefulness and the ensuing social opportunities that centre on working life. Some workers see work as an end in itself while others view it as a means to other life opportunities/openings. (Rybash *et al.* 2005)

Ethnic and Cultural Influences on the Older Person

The word ethnic is used to describe people who have a common ancestry, geographical place of origin and cultural tradition. They may share the same language, literature, music, traditions etc. Ethnic traditions are peculiar to a group of people who share a common bond.

Culture can be described as a collection of ideas and habits shared by a given group, i.e. the norms and value base of the group that help to reinforce the identity of the group, making it different from other groups. Individuals then learn the roles acceptable within their culture. (Moonie 1996)

Culture gives group members their identity, along with a sense of individuality and belonging. The United Kingdom and the United States of America are multicultural societies; Ireland is becoming increasingly so. Therefore, it is important from a health and social point of view that we demonstrate an understanding of different cultures in order to meet the needs of those who require care.

Retirement is difficult in any group, but for the increasing number of older people from other cultures who may have language difficulties, problems with religious practice and difficulty with understanding our cultures and traditions, it is extremely isolating. They may not have the same family or social network that we have. Poverty and transport difficulties may make the situation worse. We have a duty to try and correct these problems. Healthcare and social care provision will need to consider the growing problem of best providing for these constantly changing needs.

All staff in healthcare and social care settings have a duty to protect the rights of all clients in their care regardless of their cultural, religious or political beliefs. Everyone is entitled to the same level of care, to be treated with dignity and respect, and to have their cultural beliefs and practices upheld.

These cultural needs may include issues centred on diet, language and religious needs. For example, some people eat with their fingers instead of cutlery or a dress sense may be totally different to our western type of dress. Accent or language problems may lead to a lack of communication. There are occasions when an interpreter is required in order to clarify or identify needs. There may be a need to set up local day community centres so that people can have contact with others who have an understanding of their diet, dress, cultural needs and religious needs. This will provide a supportive network for like-minded groups.

In other countries older people are revered and encouraged to be active within family contexts and in other social roles. China and Japan tend to value the input of both family and community elders. More than 75 per cent of older people in Japan live with their families. The best seats on public transport are reserved for older people and people behave respectfully towards them. Some cultures, such as the Hindu culture, do not remove older people from their own homes, family and friends to put them in nursing homes. However, trends are changing – probably due to western influence.

Nowadays it is a fact of life that people may possibly end their lives in a nursing home setting. The cost of living is very high and in most families both parents work. This means that older adults requiring care are more likely to be cared for in a nursing home unit of a hospital, unless their children can afford to stay at home as full-time carers. The issue of long-term care often leads to family friction, resentment, loss of pride for the older person, as well as the isolation and sense of loss that accompanies being taken out of their environment.

Course Information

Here is a list of resources and places to go for information:

- Internet
- Local newspapers
- Libraries — books, newspapers, journals, magazines
- DVDs/videos/radio/TV
- Health centres
- Hospitals

- GP surgeries
- Chemists
- Shops e.g. health food shops
- Community centres
- Businesses
- Department of Health
- Schools
- Teachers
- Supervisors
- Fellow students
- Work colleagues
- Local councils
- Personal experience
- Personal experience of someone you know
- Previous work experience
- Registry offices for statistics and archives
- Charities
- Campaign groups
- Politicians/political parties
- Lessons
- Yellow Pages.

Useful Terms and Definitions

Health

The World Health Organization describes health as a state of complete physical, mental and social wellbeing, not merely the absence of disease or infirmity.

Physical health covers the normal functioning of the body.

Mental health covers the health of the mind and the ability to think clearly and carry out intellectual processes. It also includes the ability to express emotions and cope with mental demands like stress and worry.

Social health is the ability to form relationships, both personally and professionally. In fact, loneliness can contribute to ill health.

The three aspects (physical, mental and social) are interrelated and each can impact on the other. Therefore, the approach to health is a 'holistic' approach. An individual's state of health can have an effect on everything else they do, for example work, learning, potential and lifestyle. (Moonie 1996)

Healthy Ageing

Healthy ageing is the process by which there is a physical and psychological deterioration of body and mind. Gross motor and fine manipulative skills can be affected by loss of muscle power and bone diseases, for example arthritis whereby walking is slowed down. There are many factors that affect ageing, such as heredity, environment, lifestyle, and physical and mental health. The social impacts of ageing include retirement, lack/loss of income, family leaving home, increasing dependency, bereavement and pain/disease. All the above factors can contribute to the process of ageing 'speeding up'.

Environment

Environment means the surroundings that a person or people function in – everything that can affect people in a physical and social context. This includes air and water quality, landscape, housing and noise.

Genetic

Genetic means relating to or descriptive of an entire group or class.

Demography

Demography means the study of the characteristics of human population, such as size, growth, density, distribution and vital statistics. Demographic data means the collection of information of national or global trends.

Demographic trends are affected by population (the increase and decrease of birth and death rates), disease (the increase and eradication of diseases), emigration, immigration, diminishing labour force, war, disasters (earthquakes, tsunamis, flooding etc.), ageing population, the physically and psychologically challenged etc.

For future planning, health and social planners must consider what kind of care service elderly people will need, what kind of care elderly people will want, the type of staff who will provide these care/education needs and what kind of care government/local services will provide (dependent on economic factors).

Dementia

Dementia is a term that covers a wide range of illnesses involving the degeneration (or wasting) of the brain. Dementia is not a part of normal ageing; most very old people show no sign of this illness.

Concepts

Concepts are ways of thinking which enable people to understand and make more sense of the world. Concepts are also linguistic (language) terms used to classify, predict and explain physical and social reality. They are probably dependent on experience of events and are useful in terms of simplifying experience and for their ability to be shared with others.

Retirement

Retirement can be defined as the end of a working life. The usual retirement age in contracts of employment is 65. Retirement should be planned for and a pre-retirement course recommended. The following key areas should also be addressed: healthcare, financial provision, housing, social needs and leisure provision/social interests.

Status

A measure of the rank and prestige of a person or group of people. Status helps to define how people see themselves and how they are treated by others. Status is linked to role and different roles in a group have various levels of status attached to them.

Social Status

The value a group places on a particular social role, thus giving credibility and respect to that role, for example the leader of a group of teenagers because they can organise others or perhaps control the group through fear; a judge because of the knowledge and power to uphold the laws of society. Social status may be due to money or possessions, but these will vary depending on the culture of the groups within society.

Ethnic

The word ethnic is used to describe people who have a common ancestry, geographical place of origin and cultural tradition. They may share the same language, literature, music, traditions etc. Ethnic traditions are peculiar to a group of people who share a common bond.

Culture

Culture can be described as a collection of ideas and habits shared by a given group i.e. the norms and value base of a group. They help to reinforce the identity of the group, making it different from other groups. Individuals learn the roles acceptable to others within their culture. Cultures have their own system of values, which may be linked to religious beliefs. The culture we are raised in can be one of the biggest influences in our lives.

Values

Learned principles or systems that enable individuals to choose between alternatives and make decisions. Values guide behaviour in relation to what is judged to be 'valuable'. Values are learned in a cultural context and will develop in relation to the beliefs and norms that exist within a cultural group.

Confidentiality

The right of clients to have private information about themselves restricted to people who have an approved need of vital statistics.

Empowerment

Empowerment means giving necessary information and/or equipment/ tools that may result in giving 'control' to the client. This helps to maintain client independence and self-esteem; it allows clients to feel important and valued; and it gives clients control over their daily lives and activities, as far as possible.

In order to empower someone, it is important that the healthcare assistant's attitude is non-discriminatory. There must be respect for a client's beliefs and identity, and once decisions have been made about rights and choices, the healthcare assistant must support and uphold those choices. A client knows their own needs best and should be assisted in the identification and implementation of whatever it takes to meet those needs. It is important to maintain effective communication and confidentiality at all times.

Holistic

Holistic comes from the word holism – the theory that reality is made up of organic or unified wholes that are greater than the simple sum of their parts. Holistic means of or pertaining to holism; it emphasises the importance of the whole and the interdependence of its parts.

Cognition

Cognition is a term that refers to the mental processes involved in understanding and knowing.

Self-confidence

An individual's confidence in their own ability to achieve something or cope with a situation.

Stereotype

A way of grouping people, objects or events together and attributing individuals with the same qualities and characteristics. Stereotyping can help the individual to make sense of the world by making predictions easier. Stereotyping may have positive or negative consequences.

Ethics

The moral codes that form the basis of decision making and, therefore, the behaviour of workers in a given profession.

What Can We Do to Change the Attitude to Ageing?

- Show respect – how?
- Treat the client with dignity.
- Be an advocate and campaign for the older person's rights.
- Help maintain independence.
- Do errands for the older person, cut the grass, walk the dog etc.
- Give voluntary time in clubs/establishments.
- Take an older person to church.
- Visit residents in care settings.
- Organise events e.g. Christmas parties.

Remember that a failure in physical powers does not automatically mean a failure in psychological powers.

TASK

What else can we do?

Healthcare Assistant's Role in Promoting Positive Attitudes to Ageing

How do we look at older people in society? Do we see them as useful or useless members of society? Do they annoy us – if so, why? Do we resent them for working and perhaps holding on to jobs younger people could have? Have we got patience with their slowness or feebleness? Are we resentful of their pension/rights/benefits? Do we want the age of retirement abolished/reduced/increased?

There are a number of ways to promote positive attitudes to ageing:

- Treating the older person as a valuable member of our society who has vast knowledge and life experience.

- Recognising that a mix of younger and older workers complement each other.

- Encouraging older family members to make adequate retirement provision.

- Promoting the attendance of pre-retirement courses.

- Encouraging monetary provision for retirement.

- Promoting regular check-ups: medical and dental; smear, prostate and breast checks.

- Fostering an active mind: hobbies, reading, education etc.

- Encouraging good family and social links, such as joining clubs and encouraging friendships.

- Supporting responsible alcohol consumption: 14 units for women; 21 units for men.

- Promoting regular and active exercise: swimming, walking etc.

- Encouraging the older person to look after their appearance with good skin and hair care.

- Suggesting regular holidays.

Revision Questions

1. List some of the factors that affect the way we age.

2. What is 'demography'?

3. What influences population size?

4. What two diseases are the main killers in Ireland today?

5. As the number of older people in Ireland increases, list eight services that will need to be expanded/improved in the coming years.

6. How does our geographical location affect the healthcare that we get?

7. List four types of dementia.

8. List ten physiological signs of ageing.

9. List four psychological signs of ageing.

10. List five social changes that ageing causes.

11. List eight statutory agencies.

12. List six independent/voluntary agencies.

13. Give five reasons why retirement is so difficult for older adults.

14. What does the word 'culture' mean?

15. List three cultural needs that an older adult from another country may have in an Irish hospital/nursing home.

16. Write down three ways to promote positive attitudes to ageing.

Chapter 2

Working with the Older Person

Chapter Outline

- Needs of the older person
- Role of the healthcare assistant
- Communicating effectively
- Empowerment
- Advocacy
- Independence
- Individualised care
- Dignity
- Choice
- Respect
- Self-esteem
- Including family/carers as partners in care
- Personal effectiveness in the workplace
- Health promotion for older clients
- Therapeutic interventions

Needs of the Older Person

A need is an essential requirement, which must be satisfied in order to help an individual achieve or restore (if lost) an acceptable level of social independence or quality of life. (Moonie 2007)

Maslow's Hierarchy of Needs

Needs can be:

- Physical
- Social
- Emotional
- Psychological
- Recreational
- Financial
- Environmental
- Spiritual.

Social Needs

Social health includes the ability to form and maintain relationships, both personally and professionally. During life it is almost impossible to live in isolation, so human beings must learn to interact and form relationships. Social health is a very important aspect of health. If social needs are not met, loneliness and isolation result. These emotions can have a negative effect on mental health. Some needs are just as important in a care setting as they are in a client's home.

Emotional Needs

Emotional needs relate to the human need to feel loved and nurtured, and to have a close bond with other people. Everyone has this need. Emotional needs are centred on the feelings of the individual and their ability to express or support these feelings. How emotions are expressed depend upon social, cultural and environmental aspects. Happiness, anger, sadness and distress are easily recognisable emotions. Older people are a vulnerable group and their emotional needs are often neglected.

Psychological Needs

Psychology is to do with the mind and the study of its processes. Therefore, it is to do with mental wellbeing – often physical deterioration has an effect on mental wellbeing. Mental wellbeing is the ability to think clearly, problem solve, make rational decisions and perform particular processes to do with the intellect. It also includes the ability to express emotions, deal with stressful situations and cope with other demands on the mind.

Intellectual needs refer to the need to keep the brain active. Mental alertness can be stimulated by interests and hobbies. As physical capabilities fail, it is very important to keep up an interest in various activities to enhance and expand mental agility.

Social, physical, mental, emotional and intellectual health are all interlinked and have an effect on each other. Complete social, physical, mental, emotional and intellectual health does not just mean to be well physically; one can be well physically but have an emotional problem that affects one's mental health. This is taking a holistic view of health i.e. all needs are interlinked.

Recreational Needs

A recreational need is a need for mental activity or stimulation. This includes interests/activities that can be done in the client's spare time and that can be done anywhere, for example in hospital, a nursing home or the client's own home.

Recreational activities stimulate physical, mental and emotional wellbeing. It is important to note that while there can be a progressive deterioration in a client's physical capabilities, a positive effort should be made to meet their recreational needs regardless.

Activities should be suitable for the client group, i.e. they should be age and skills appropriate, and they should evoke a good response. An activity programme should have client input as they know their needs and likes/dislikes best.

Financial Needs

Older people may be financially dependent if they are in a lower socio-economic group or if they have made no pension provision. There is a state pension payable to those aged over 65, but that amount may not meet their needs – often older people may have to decide between fuel and food.

If a client cannot deal with their own affairs, then appropriate legal steps must be taken to ensure that someone else can do it for them. An assessment of cognitive skills, mental ability and understanding are carried out by a GP, and a referral to a medical consultant specialising in care of the older person will be made if deemed necessary. Power of attorney is a legal process giving power to one person (a relative/professional person) to conduct another person's financial affairs. On occasion a social service department can (under guardianship arrangements) assume responsibility. This allows them to write cheques, assist with paying bills and deal with other financial commitments.

Environmental Needs

Environmental means relating to the surroundings in which we live. Environmental includes housing, noise, air and water quality, and landscape. In fact, it refers to anything that affects people's existence in a physical and social context. Environmental needs in a hospital or nursing home setting are closely related to physical needs i.e. warmth, temperature, food, drinks, friendliness, quiet and atmosphere.

People should wherever possible be cared for in their own surroundings. Homecare can be achieved through the help of family/friends, or through the assistance of community care packages, which are generally organised by a public health nurse. Community care packages usually require input from a GP, community/public health nurse, an occupational therapist, physiotherapist, social worker and family members.

Other areas that can potentially have input include Meals on Wheels, home help services, a nurse/carer (input with washing, dressing and physical needs) and the assistance of family/friends. The local housing department will make adjustments to the dwelling place, for example ramps, shower and stair lift. The client should be involved in all the decisions made about their care.

Spiritual Needs

Spiritual needs have to do with beliefs. One of the basic human rights is the freedom of thought, conscience and religious expression. As healthcare assistants we have a duty to facilitate all religious beliefs as Ireland becomes a multicultural society. We must be prepared to learn about different cultures and religions, and be able to assist clients to practise their religion in our care environment.

How Can Spiritual Needs Be Met?

- Identify religious denomination and learn how to facilitate it.

- Ask clients to state what their religious needs might be.

- Create an environment of peace and quiet for religious practice.

- Treat all ministers of religion with dignity and respect.

- Facilitate groups/people who want to pray together.

- Have religious symbols ready for use e.g. candles, crucifix, rosary beads and white cloth.

- Remind clients about mass on the TV.

- Accompany Eucharistic ministers on visits to give Holy Communion to sick clients in rooms.

- Ensure that dying clients have the Sacrament of the Sick (if they wish).

Religious practices are private and personal. We have no right to try and change beliefs or push our beliefs onto somebody else. People who are spiritually fulfilled are generally happy and accepting.

Role of the Healthcare Assistant

The role of the healthcare assistant is to assist the registered nurse to carry out planned care, to have an understanding of what needs to be reported/recorded, to report any unusual findings to the registered nurse and to carry out basic 'care of the person' duties i.e. head-to-toe care – skin, body, hair, eye, mouth and hand nail care.

The healthcare assistant will assist with the following tasks:

- Grooming

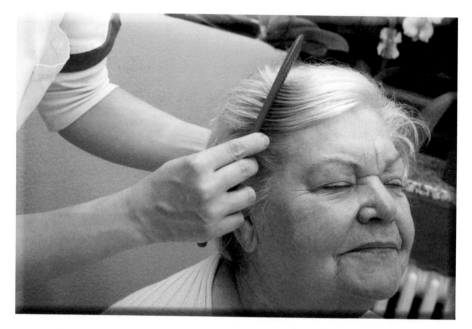

- Washing and dressing
- Mobility
- Continence needs
- Eating and drinking
- Facilitating a good sleep pattern
- Social/recreational activities (sometimes participating in those activities)
- Encouraging independence in all aspects of care.

The healthcare assistant may also have to orientate the client to time and place, read the daily programme of events and relevant newspaper information, and assist in watching current affairs or news on TV to help them keep up with what is happening locally and worldwide.

The healthcare assistant should:

- Know how to communicate effectively with all types of clients in their care.

- Know about confidentiality and how to ensure it.

- Have enthusiasm for their job.

- Be able to interpret the non-verbal messages of vulnerable clients i.e. know the 'norms' for each client.

- Be cheerful in the execution of duties and tasks.

- Never show disapproval when doing a task that is difficult or repugnant.

- Be a good listener.

- Not appear 'rushed' if someone wants to tell them something, which may be important to them.

Communicating Effectively

Communication is a two-way process: there is a sender and a receiver of a message. Some clients may feel vulnerable and have a basic feeling of insecurity about what may happen to them in a care setting. It is important to eradicate fear and create an environment where clients feel physically and emotionally safe.

Communication can be verbal (what is said) and non-verbal (the use of body language). We often use more than words to say what we mean: our non-verbal messages can enhance or detract from what we say. Our eyes or our bodies are used in non-verbal communication.

People who suffer from certain disabilities may have difficulties with communication. People with hearing difficulties will rely heavily on non-verbal communication. They can often lip read which means they will closely observe facial expressions and lip movements to decipher words. They usually manage to understand communication through close observation of body and sign language.

People with vision difficulties have the disadvantage of not being able to read facial expressions or see body movements. They cannot recognise people by sight. They have to rely heavily on hearing skills such as listening to the tone of voice and picking out various meanings of what is being said.

Braille is a touch system for people who cannot see. Words are formed into raised dots and read by touch of fingers rather than visually. Often computers and books with large print can be used for the partially sighted.

For those with speech difficulties an electronic board called a 'Bliss system' is often used. Different words or phrases, which the person may require, are on the board and they point to the one that they need.

Communication with the client will involve assessing their problem and deciding on the method of communication best suited to assisting in their expression of need. The client must be considered about all aspects of their care. Families should also be included. Both parties know best what is required and can make valuable suggestions on how care goals can be achieved.

Effective communication can be facilitated by:

- Showing sympathy/empathy to both client and family/friends.
- Being prepared to listen to problems and assist in finding solutions.
- Using open body language so that you appear approachable.
- Being friendly, smiling and showing a caring attitude.

Remember that confidential information must not be abused. If asked questions where confidentiality may be breached, refer the person to a trained member of staff who can assist. Healthcare assistants are not allowed to reveal any client details to anyone at any time.

Some other recommendations for effective communication include being polite to members of the multi-disciplinary team and assisting wherever you can. The healthcare assistant should also know how to answer the telephone properly as sometimes callers can be put off by an unhelpful answer to a call. Take accurate information from a caller and get them to repeat anything that is unclear; refer the contents of the call to the relevant person.

Empowerment

Empowerment means giving control to the client. It involves enabling them to take control of their own lives, make their own decisions and choose their own activities. Traditionally health professionals acted as experts, making decisions based on information collected about the client or from the client. Decisions were made by the professionals with little or no input from the client, which put them in a 'passive' rather than an 'active' position.

Nowadays it is understood that people are experts on themselves. They know their own physical, emotional, psychological, social, spiritual and cognitive needs. Therefore, power should rightfully rest with the client.

In a case where a client has difficulty or lacks confidence, then power can be 'shared' between the client and the healthcare assistant. The relationship is better when there is mutual trust and understanding, where the healthcare assistant shows patience and empathy, and where dignity and privacy are respected. If a difficulty exists collecting information from the client, friends or family may be able to provide valuable information about personal needs, and cultural or background information about a client's lifestyle, beliefs or aspirations.

To enable empowerment of the client, there needs to be effective communication and interaction, and respect for religious and other beliefs. The right to make choices or decisions should rest with the client and this should happen in a 'safe' (psychological and physical safety), non-discriminatory environment. By giving the client the information, skills and equipment/tools necessary to enable them to lead as independent a life as possible is to empower them.

Advocacy

Being an advocate means representing the interests of another by speaking on their behalf and presenting their case for them. Advocacy also means encouraging and enabling clients to speak up for themselves and be assertive. People who require advocacy are usually vulnerable members of society, for example children, sick people, poorer members of society and ethnic minorities. Very sick clients often need the nurse to act as an advocate if they feel unable to make their wishes known or have them respected. Clients with disability, sickness, language or other communication problems often find it difficult to express their needs. Encouraging clients to self-express is assisting with self-advocacy and it is also a way of empowering them.

Independence

This is the ability to do things for oneself without help or assistance from anyone else. It means being able to control one's own environment, lifestyle and choices, and fulfil one's needs.

Being dependent may feel like a burden to some clients, who often 'fiercely' defend their independent status. Healthcare assistants should be encouraged to do for the clients only what they cannot do for themselves in order to help maintain their independence. Decision making should always involve the client and family.

An assessment of needs is necessary and is done to find out what areas of care the client needs assistance with. Discussion is important as healthcare assistants need to listen to and interact with the client in order to best identify their care needs.

Allowing sufficient time to perform tasks is really important, as there may be a loss of dignity and confidence if actions are rushed. A skills assessment is necessary also, as equipment/tools to perform basic tasks may be required. Knowledge of a client's past lifestyle helps the healthcare assistant to better identify a client's needs and interact in a more therapeutic and compassionate manner with the client.

Individualised Care

Individualised care is specifically designed for a particular client. We are all individuals with our own likes and dislikes. Each of us has different personalities, with moral, religious and cultural beliefs which make us all unique. Individualised care involves the delivery of care by using a recognised care model such as the Roper, Logan and Tierney Model of Nursing. This model describes the 12 Activities of Daily Living, which will be dealt with in more detail later on in this module.

The 12 Activities of Daily Living

1. Maintaining a safe environment

2. Communication

3. Breathing and circulation

4. Eating and drinking (nutrition)

5. Elimination

6. Washing and dressing

7. Controlling body temperature

8. Mobilisation

9. Working and playing (social interaction)

10. Expressing sexuality

11. Sleeping

12. Dying

A nurse determines the individual care needs of each client on admission. A care plan is then written. The nurse sets realistic/achievable goals and then plans a review date of the care plan after 3/6 months, or as necessary (if the condition changes, improves or deteriorates). All care plans should be legible, signed, dated and properly filed – they are legal documents that must be kept for seven years.

Dignity

Processing self-esteem, feeling worthy of respect and showing pride in oneself are all components of dignity. Dignity is quite a fragile concept and preserving it can be difficult. There needs to be mutual respect between clients and healthcare assistants. Tasks, especially intimate ones, should be performed in a private setting and the minimum number of people required for the task should be present. A notice should be put on the door to ensure privacy as well as to preserve dignity.

Clients' feelings and desires should be known and encouragement given to express them. Prompts, encouragers and confidence boosters should be used appropriately and frequently.

Tasks that may be distasteful for the healthcare assistant should be carried out tactfully and the healthcare assistant's distaste must not be made known to the client. This distaste can be displayed through adverse body language or disapproving glances or gestures. Clients should be spoken to and not spoken over, and they should be spoken to as adults and not spoken down to or patronised. Lack of patience can also lead to loss of dignity.

Choice

As individuals we can make our own decisions about what we want, how we live, where we socialise, the type of work we do, who to be with, where to go etc. The ability to choose gives us a sense of self-respect and self-worth. Everyone has a right to make choices and as healthcare assistants we cannot disregard a client's wishes, unless it is obvious that a client does not have the cognitive/mental capacity to make the decision/choice. For example, take a client with severe dementia who does not want a carer to change an incontinence pad even though it is heavily soiled. In cases like this it may be necessary to override the client's decision if it is not felt to be in their best interests.

Nevertheless, we should 'enable' or 'facilitate' the client wherever possible. If the client is vulnerable because of illness, confusion or lack of confidence, the people who know them best should be included in their care. Family and friends can help us make the best choice with/for them.

By facilitating client choice, we demonstrate respect and, in doing so, help preserve dignity. Allow mistakes and give options/alternatives to the client. Give information and provide the means, such as skills/equipment, to enable the client to make the best decisions/choices.

Constraints on Choice

Loss of dignity may create vulnerability, as the amount of help required or assistance needed may be great. The client may feel that their emotions or feelings are being ignored and may find that they have a lack of confidence and self-esteem. The attitude of the care deliverer should be one of encouragement. Healthcare assistants should facilitate choice and be non-discriminatory, as discrimination causes disadvantages.

Lack of patience and body language that conveys impatience, i.e. standing with hand on hip, looking upwards, looking at watch etc., puts pressure on clients and makes them feel burdensome. Healthcare assistants should always be patient with clients and not rush them. They should never criticise a client's choice, as this can be patronising.

Ways to Facilitate Choice

- Allowing choice of menu at mealtimes.
- Permitting flexibility of mealtimes or where meals are taken e.g. in privacy of room, in dining room or in a quiet corner.
- Letting clients choose their own clothing.
- Encouraging choice of bedtime, nap times and bath times.
- Giving time to the older person to express feelings and identify needs.
- Asking clients' opinions about choice of entertainment.
- Allowing clients to assist in formulating their own care plan.

Respect

Dignity means being worthy of respect, and possessing pride and self-esteem. Dignity and respect go hand in hand. In order to preserve dignity, people must be given respect. Respect means treating each person as an individual, tolerating their point of view, allowing and facilitating choice and generally treating people the way that we would like to be treated ourselves. Respect should be shown to all clients regardless of background, illness, personality etc. Always remember the golden rule: do unto others what you would have others do unto you. Everyone should be treated with respect.

Self-esteem

Self-esteem refers to self-worth. A person's level of self-esteem reflects the level of love, respect and pride they have for themselves. Everyone has a different level of self-esteem. Healthcare assistants should remember that illness and dependency usually decrease a person's self-esteem as clients begin to doubt their abilities, lose faith in themselves and feel useless, helpless and burdensome.

We can help clients to maintain a good level of self-esteem by encouraging them to focus on the positives in their lives; to concentrate on the things that they can do instead of what they cannot. We can also help by encouraging them to take an interest in their lives, get involved in their care, take pride in their appearance and participate in social activities. Increasing self-esteem can lead to a boost in confidence and self-worth which makes a client a happier person. Low self-esteem can lead to a lack of confidence which can result in depression and unhappiness.

Including Family/Carers as Partners in Care

Older people are a vulnerable group. If they have their full faculties, they can make their own decisions regarding their care needs. If not, family/

friends can help by giving some background knowledge on the client's previous lifestyle, job and family. Clients know their own needs best and should be consulted about every aspect of their care.

Family/friends can also play a valuable part in the client's care. If they are aware of problems and solutions are suggested, they often become actively involved. They may then decide to play a part in feeding, mobilising, washing, dressing or helping the older person to socialise. Involving families in the client's care gives them a sense of value and worth as they feel that they are still useful to their loved one and that they play some role in their care.

Family involvement in care makes clients feel loved and alleviates feelings of abandonment, which some older adults experience when they realise that they are being cared for, solely, by strangers in a nursing home or hospital. Family involvement in care has its advantages for healthcare assistants also. It gives them additional time for other work or other clients who do not have family/friends that visit.

Personal Effectiveness in the Workplace

Personal effectiveness is enhanced or affected by the following aspects in the workplace:

Purpose/aim: Healthcare assistants need to have a purpose or aim within the work setting. In the caring service, healthcare assistants work as part of a team to provide assistance, support and personal care for older people in a loving, caring environment. Team performance requires constant motivation and reinforcement. If goals or outcomes are not identified clearly, tasks are performed aimlessly and patient care and staff morale is affected by lack of motivation.

Job-specific training: A knowledge of what to do and why it is being done in a particular way is important. Well-trained staff deliver better care. If healthcare assistants feel that they are achieving personal goals, learning different skills and being intellectually challenged, they are most likely to remain motivated and be effective in the workplace.

Being a member of the unit team: Feeling part of a group with shared goals and desired outcomes can keep people motivated, effective and productive.

Responsibility: Having a specific purpose, role and degree of responsibility suited to one's abilities can make people feel valued and challenged. It can also increase overall personal effectiveness.

Poor staffing levels: Sufficient staff numbers to perform the required tasks and communicate adequately with clients is another factor necessary for personal effectiveness. Staff cannot do what is required as well as it should be done if there is not sufficient staff. Poor staffing levels cause increases in sickness and accident rates, and frustration and exhaustion in staff which inevitably affects patient care.

Staff relationships: If staff members respect one another and value each other's input, working life will be easier. If they share information, have positive attitudes and try to work together as a team, it will improve their effectiveness as individuals. Clients can see, hear and sense unrest among staff members and it does usually affect some aspect of their care. So, an effort should be made to get along, but if people cannot, they should try to be professional and put their differences aside for the sake of work or not work opposite one another, if absolutely necessary.

Good communication: Healthcare assistants should be encouraged to take part in handovers at shift changes. They may have contributions to make, as they tend to spend most of their time with patients during the duration of their shifts. They should also be given any relevant information about patients so that they can do their job efficiently, such as new residents, discharges, infectious diseases, pressure area changes and family/social circumstances.

Praise: Everyone needs positive reinforcement to feel respected and valued.

Suggestions: If something can be done better, quicker or more efficiently, the healthcare assistant should not be afraid to suggest it.

Camaraderie: A sense of teamwork and commitment helps staff to support each other in the workplace. The best teams consist of caring, genuine, warm, loyal and compassionate individuals. Good teamwork is vital for effective care delivery.

Constraints: Aggressive, domineering and controlling colleagues, who disallow the sharing of points of view, can affect the team and its overall effectiveness.

Negativity: Always identifying problems and the negative side of things affect staff morale. Negativity should only be shared in very small doses! Remember: is the glass half full or half empty?

Lack/loss of confidence: Confidence needs to be built up and constantly reinforced. Good managers and supportive colleagues will be able to do this easily.

Health Promotion for Older Clients

Health promotion is the activity of promoting healthy choices and health improvements. It contributes to a number of factors:

- General wellbeing
- Emotional wellbeing
- A 'feel good' factor
- Identification of health-related problems
- Improvement of body function
- Uptake of exercise regime/fitness
- Longevity.

In older people it is important to promote a healthy attitude towards the following aspects:

Healthy eating: Healthy eating means knowing what constitutes a healthy diet. It constitutes drinking lots of fluids and taking a well-balanced high-fibre, low-fat type of diet. The older person's diet should consist of a balance of proteins, carbohydrates, dairy products, fruit and vegetables, and oils/fats. All the above foods are contained in the food pyramid. A balance of these foods should keep the body healthy. Older people have no need to diet unless there is a medical reason.

At least two litres of fluid should be taken in order to promote healthy urinary output, promote good skin integrity, prevent urinary tract problems and keep constipation at bay. Also, the older person may need to have the healthy options of food presented in a different way to make the eating process easier, for example stewed apples as opposed to whole apples.

Fruit and vegetables: At last five portions per day ensures good bowel function.

Adequate portions of protein: Protein is a cell repairer so meat, eggs, beans and oily fish should be taken.

Dairy produce (calcium): Milk, yoghurt and cheese.

Carbohydrates: Bread, cereals, potatoes (all taken in moderation).

Oils: Essential in small quantities; preferably polyunsaturated fats to prevent cholesterol build-up.

Alcohol consumption: Alcohol should be taken in moderation and the guidelines for alcohol consumption adhered to: 14 units for women; 21 units for men. However, older people should take less because their body bulk is lighter. They also take medication which may interact with the alcohol. For safety reasons, they shouldn't be encouraged to drink at home or if they are alone.

Exercise: Older people need exercise. Twenty minutes exercise three times per week is recommended. Forms of suitable exercise for older people include walking, swimming, dancing, and upper body and lower body exercise. Swimming and walking are especially excellent forms of exercise. Exercise helps maintain muscle tone and flexibility. If muscle tone is enhanced, it helps to improve joint function. The positive effects of exercise include the following:

- Increased muscle strength/lung strength.
- Increased cardiac activities/lower blood pressure.
- Increased urinary output/efficiency.
- Improved co-ordination.
- Increased flexibility and decreased stiffness.
- Prevention of build-up of cholesterol deposits.
- Keeps obesity at bay.

There is also the psychological 'bonus' of exercise; the increased 'feel-good factor', which means there is less chance of developing problems like anxiety/depression.

Smoking: Smoking has a detrimental effect on all the major organs and should be discouraged in all cases. Health promotion days may show clients that smoking is harmful. However, clients have choice and if a client chooses to smoke despite the warning, we must respect that choice and facilitate it by allowing them to access designated smoking areas and bringing them there, if necessary.

Medical abuse: Older adults should be educated about their medications, side-effects and reasons for their use. This will help avoid any abuse of medication and the associated problems this abuse can cause.

Self-care: Good hygiene habits, being clean and well presented, taking care of skin, and regular dental visits and eye tests as the adult gets older help highlight apparent problems as they present.

Voluntary work: Voluntary work can help the retired person make new friends, feel useful and give them something positive to do, thus increasing their confidence.

Therapeutic Interventions

There are therapeutic interventions that can improve/enhance the social interaction of older people. However, there are often constraints that prevent older adults from accessing such social activities. These constraints include transport issues, personal issues and a lack of a support network.

Transport issues can mean that the older person lives in the country/out of town and there is poor public transport, and wheelchair taxi networks are costly and unaffordable for pensioners. The client may be feeble and have no family or friends to transport them. Personal issues include the client being elderly, feeble, in pain, depressed/confused, nervous/afraid, or having a lack/loss of mental/intellectual skills. A lack of support may mean the client has no one to accompany them and is unable to go alone. Perhaps they could go if they had a carer.

Therapeutic interventions include:

Day care: Having access to a group of people their own age, enjoying conversation, having a hot meal, playing games, taking part in an exercise regime, becoming involved in music sessions/dance and possibly having a bath/shower. It may be possible to organise chiropodist/hairdresser visits also.

Speech therapy: This is difficult to access or there is limited access. After the initial session of assessment there is often insufficient follow-up.

Occupational therapy: This is useful for helping mental stimulation. Occupational therapy is often attached to hospitals.

Physiotherapy: There is limited access, too few therapists and the older person may have to pay through private healthcare.

Chiropody: People with foot problems would benefit from frequent chiropody. Problems include ingrown toenails, bunions, corns etc. Chiropody can be costly. Appropriately-designed and fitted footwear can help mobility.

Alternative therapy: There are alternative medicines/therapies that can enhance conventional medicine. These include: massage, which is comforting/soothing; hydrotherapy involving warm aromatic baths and salts; reflexology, which is a form of massage of (mainly) hands/feet and is beneficial; reiki, which is centred on universal life energy; yoga, which is considered a way of life, affecting the whole person; aromatherapy involving the use of concentrated oils; and acupuncture, which is an attempt to balance the force in the body that causes ailments/disease.

Revision Questions

1. List the types of needs that human beings have.

2. What is meant by 'power of attorney'?

3. List six ways that the older adult's spiritual needs can be met.

4. List some of the qualities healthcare assistants working with older adults should possess.

5. What is 'Braille'?

6. List four ways that healthcare assistants can communicate more effectively.

7. Define 'empowerment'.

8. What is an 'advocate'?

9. What is meant by 'individual care'?

10. List the 12 Activities of Daily Living.

11. List three ways that healthcare assistants can help to maintain a client's dignity.

12. List three constraints on preserving dignity.

13. List four ways that healthcare assistants can facilitate choice for the client.

14. What is 'respect'?

15. What is 'self-esteem'?

16. List eight ways that personal effectiveness can be enhanced in the workplace.

17. List four main ways that healthcare assistants can promote health in the older adult.

Chapter 3

Caring for Older People with Specific Needs

Chapter Outline

- Identifying and adapting care and practices.

- Cognitive impairment and the older person.

- Sensory impairment and the older person.

- Mental illness and the older person.

- Conditions in an older person that require immediate attention.

- Impact of living with chronic illness.

- Individual needs of the dying older person and their family.

- Respectfully carrying out duties after death.

Identifying and Adapting Care and Practices

Cognition is the term used to describe the mental processes that are involved in knowing, understanding, perceiving and thinking. Mental abilities have the potential to improve as people get older, provided they are continuously used. There is some evidence to suggest that mental ability declines if it is not used/tested. This means that mental exercises and stimulation are just as important for the older person as physical exercises. Therefore, nurses and healthcare assistants have an obligation to identify and adapt care and practices in order to provide mental stimulation for clients in their care.

Cognitive Impairment and the Older Person

People suffering from dementia have cognitive impairment; their memory is impaired. Initially short-term memory declines but eventually long-term memory is also affected. Care and practice need to be adapted so that the needs of the client with cognitive impairment can be met. The client will require a clutter-free, safe environment and may require constant orientation to person, time and place. A higher level of concentration and patience is required when caring for people with cognitive needs. A client with dementia should be allocated a bedroom near the nurses' station; this can assist both clients and staff to maintain a safe environment.

Clients with dementia require mental stimulation and social interaction. This can be achieved in a number of ways:

- Taking the client out for a walk can help to relieve stress at being indoors, as walking is both therapeutic and good exercise.

- Sitting outdoors around the garden tables.

- Introduce snoezelen therapy for visual and sensual stimulation.

- Place flowers around the care setting for visual beauty and scent/ aroma.

- Introduce a fish tank as swimming fish have a therapeutic effect.

- Introduce musical activity and reminiscence tapes.

- Set up the idea of animal visits as older people love animals.

Sensory Impairment and the Older Person

Bedrooms should be user-friendly. The blind/partially sighted can use a clock system to identify object positions in rooms. This involves entering a room and remembering that the window is straight ahead (12 o'clock), the bed is to the right (3 o'clock) and so on. It is for this reason it is important that things are left in the same place and lockers/bed tables are clutter-free. Allow the client to count the paces to the toilet/door/window. An alarm buzzer should be placed within reach of the client whenever they are alone. Talk regularly to clients with sight impairments about their environment to help them understand where they are, who they are sitting with etc. Enquire whether or not the local library supplies audio, Braille and large print books.

When caring for clients with sight impairments, always knock on entering their room, introduce yourself and ask permission to do whatever it is you have come to do. Give options to the client and always have patience. Remember: even if people cannot see you, their other senses are heightened and they can hear long sighs and sense impatience.

Most clients with a hearing impairment can lip read, so speak clearly and DO NOT SHOUT. Some can read sign language; others will use notepads to communicate, requesting that staff write down what they wish to say. Other clients with hearing impairments wear hearing aids. For those wearing hearing aids, staff should ensure that batteries are replaced when required, ears are free from wax and the client wears the aid.

When dealing with clients with all types of hearing impairments, always be patient, make good eye contact, identify individual needs and use good body language. Remember: clients need to communicate so any aids they have for this must be in good working order.

Mental Illness and the Older Person

Mental health means the absence of mental illness. It also means the ability of the individual to deal with life's trials and traumas in an efficient and reasonable manner. It involves using coping mechanisms that show an accurate perception of reality. Mental illness covers social and emotional disability and also covers the following illnesses:

- Anxiety
- Depression (endogenous and reactive/exogenous)
- Manic depressive psychosis
- Schizophrenia
- Dementia.

People with mental illness have needs that can be best identified by examining Roper, Logan and Tierney's Activities of Daily Living and Maslow's Hierarchy of Needs. These models cover the physical, psychological and emotional needs of the client.

Maintaining a safe environment: There are many issues related to maintaining a safe environment for the older person with mental illness, for example wandering behaviour. Constant aimless wandering and attempts to leave the building or enter other patients' rooms need to be monitored. There is a lack of understanding of danger or no concept of danger. Slips, trips and falls are more common; smoking is a hazard; electrical appliances and sharp or hot objects (kettles, cookers etc.) can also be hazardous. The client may invade the personal space of other clients who may get angry.

Communication: People with mental illness may have difficulty communicating. They may be withdrawn, talk to 'voices', out of touch with reality, suffer from hallucinations/delusions. Their responses can be passive/unresponsive i.e. they may have a lack of understanding of what is being said to them or not care either way. If they don't understand, there may be difficulty with co-operation and they can become resistant or aggressive. Explain all procedure in clear, concise language and if a client gets particularly stressed or aggressive, leave them for a while and come back to them.

Personal care: People with mental illness often self-neglect because they may have lost the ability to care for themselves. They neglect general appearance and put clothing on in the wrong order, for example vest over clothing, nightwear with overcoat or slippers with suit. This shows a loss of automatic skills (learned in childhood). When this is the case, they will need to be washed, dressed and groomed by staff.

Continence: Incontinence can cause a loss of dignity. Clients may be embarrassed/ashamed of incontinence wear, such as pads, and they may pull it off. Staff should anticipate needs and be able to read client 'body language'. If they appear to be looking for the toilet, take or direct them. A client's skin should be washed and dried after using the toilet or after a pad change.

Eating and drinking: The ability to eat independently may be lost due to a loss of appetite or concentration. Clients may slop/spill food, and in these cases, clients should be supervised or fed during mealtimes. Adequate nutrition levels need to be maintained and weights taken regularly. It is often a better idea to bring clients with similar eating/drinking needs to an area to eat together, as it can be difficult for independent clients to witness and embarrassing for patients to be fed in front of others. Dignity should be preserved.

Spiritual needs: A minister of religion will visit the care setting, if required. Spiritual needs and other appropriate spiritual practices should be catered for.

Mobilising: Clients suffering from mental illness may feel unable to mobilise as their mobility decreases; others may walk or 'pace' through the nursing home. They may walk into objects or persons in their path. The walking may appear to be purposeful but there is no set destination – just aimless wandering. The environment should be safe and clutter-free from obstacles to prevent slips and trips. The use of a hip protector should be considered if a client is mobile but prone to falling. However, always refer to the local policy in the care setting.

Walking and playing: Sometimes it is difficult to get people to sit or become involved during planned activities due to lack of attention span or comprehension. Activities should be person-centred and designed to suit each client's needs. Activities can include walking, nail care, hand massage, snoezelen therapy, music, film, bingo, quizzes, yoga and movement to music.

Sleeping: Sleep is so important. Cell repair takes place during sleep and our bodies require 7½ hours' sleep each night. Lack of sleep causes clients to be sleepy the next day, when they need to be alert in order to eat, drink and mobilise adequately. Clients with illness are often restless during the night. It often takes a long time for them to go to sleep and then they may wake very early in the morning. This can result in difficult behaviours both during the night and the following day, which can cause clients to feel exhausted, aggressive and resistant. Therefore, it is important to establish a good sleep pattern. Medication may be required. An improved sleep pattern should result in an improvement in behaviour.

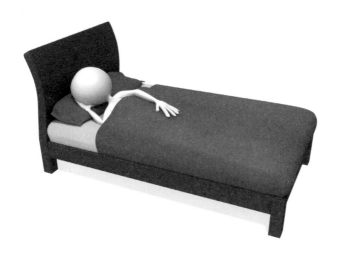

Expressing sexuality: Often there is inappropriate sexual behaviour because of an inability to express sexuality in an appropriate manner. Nurses and healthcare assistants have an obligation to protect the client's dignity if they are unable to do this for themselves.

Other issues can include the following:

Inappropriate behaviour: This includes behaviour that is not suitable for time or place. Clients who behave inappropriately are often those who are mentally ill and suffer from confused states. Some examples of inappropriate behaviour include undressing incorrectly, inappropriate dressing, urinating in public places, 'pacing' up and down, wandering behaviour during the night and inappropriate eating habits, such as grabbing food or eating with their hands.

Emotional responses: Often emotions are mixed up e.g. crying/laughing at the wrong time. Things that are normally considered serious can appear quite funny, often causing embarrassment to the family.

Financial problems: The client often forgets/loses their purse, wallet or handbag. They can accuse carers or family of stealing. They often lose valuables, jewellery, car or house keys and may even hide things for protection, but forget they've done this and accuse people of taking them. Again, this can cause distress and embarrassment to carers and family.

Stigma

There is stigma attached to mental illness. Often people with mental illness are shunned, called inappropriate names and treated unequally by society. Large mental hospitals have, on the whole, ceased to exist and small units attached to general hospitals have been the trend for the past 20 years or so. The majority of mentally ill people are cared for in the community with psychiatric community nurses to support them. However, it is sad that a lot of mentally ill patients end up in prison or shelters for the homeless.

Dementia

Dementia is a broad term used to describe a group of symptoms caused by disorders that affect the brain. These symptoms include:

- Confusion with time or place.

- Memory loss which disrupts daily life.

- Challenges in planning or solving problems.

- Changes in mood or personality.

- Withdrawal from work or social activities.

- Misplacing things or losing the ability to retrace steps.

- Trouble understanding visual images.

- Poor judgment.

- Difficulty completing familiar tasks.

- New problems with words when speaking or writing.

Many dementias are progressive; this means that they start out slowly and gradually get worse. Dementia is caused by damage to brain cells. This damage interferes with the ability of the brain cells to communicate with each other and this affects thinking, behaviour and feelings. While over 100 different diseases will produce symptoms of dementia, Alzheimer's disease is the most common dementia and accounts for more than 50 per cent of all cases. The other more common types are vascular dementia and Parkinson's disease.

There is no one test to determine if someone has dementia. Doctors diagnose Alzheimer's and other dementias based on medical/family history, physical examination, blood tests, memory testing and establishing day-to-day functional ability. In some cases a brain scan may be ordered to make sure that the symptoms are not caused by a problem unrelated to dementia.

Dementia is more common in older people, but sometimes it can start in people as young as 40 years old. About 10–15 per cent of people over the age of 65 have some form of dementia and about 20 per cent (1 in 5) will have some degree of it by the age of 80. People can live with dementia anywhere from 2 years to 20 years. In Ireland it is estimated that some 40,000 people have dementia; this will increase to over 100,000 in the next 30 years.

In the case of the most progressive dementias, including Alzheimer's disease, there is no cure and no treatment which slows or stops its progression. However, there are drug treatments, which can be discussed with a doctor, that may temporarily improve troubling symptoms. In recent years conventional beliefs and treatments of Alzheimer's disease have been re-examined with a new focus being placed on using a person-centred approach to care.

Support Services

- Alzheimer Society of Ireland
  FREEPHONE: 1800 341 341
  Email: info@alzheimer.ie

- The Carers Association
  FREEPHONE: 1800 24 07 24
  Email: info@carersireland.com

- Dementia Services Information and Development Centre
  Tel.: 01 416 2035
  Email: dsidc@stjames.ie

Conditions Requiring Immediate Attention

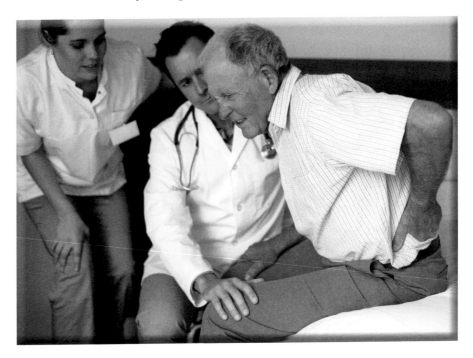

Within a healthcare setting, nurses deal with medical emergencies. The healthcare assistant should be able to recognise emergencies and understand the need for immediate nurse input; they must only do what they can do safely: summon help immediately, reassure the client, deal with any upset caused to onlookers by the incident and make the surrounding area 'safe'. **Note:** never do anything that can have a detrimental impact on you, the nurse on duty or your employer. Do only what you have been sufficiently trained to do.

Emergencies are situations that require immediate attention:

- Cardiac arrest (heart attack)
- Shock (sudden drop in blood pressure)
- Choking
- Difficulty with breathing

- Fractures
- Epileptic seizure
- Loss of consciousness
- Burns and scalds
- Electric shock
- Poisoning
- Severe bleeding.

Cardiac Arrest

Causes: Heart attack, shock, convulsion, electric shock, other injuries.

Check for: Pulse/no pulse, breathing stopped.

Action: Summon help immediately.

Shock

Causes: Sudden drop in blood pressure due to bleeding, severe burns (loss of skin, loss of fluid), vomiting, diarrhoea (loss of circulating body fluid), heart attack.

Check for: Colour is pale/white/grey; skin is cold, clammy and sweaty; pulse is fast/weak/thready; breathing is fast and/or shallow; may feel nauseous and vomit.

Action: Summon help immediately.

Choking

Causes: Poor swallowing reflex; piece of food/foreign object stuck at back of throat.

Check for: Face congestion – red face, bulging eyes; face later turns grey if obstruction still there; may be unable to breathe; may point to throat.

Action: Summon nurse urgently. Obstruction must be removed quickly.

Difficulty with Breathing

Causes: Asthma, heart attack, chest disease, choking, seizure, airway obstruction, poisoning.

Check for: Fear; change in breathing pattern; any visible obstructions.

Action: Summon help immediately.

Fractures

Causes: A fracture is a crack or break in a bone, usually as a result of a fall.

Check for: Swelling; complaints of pain at site of injury; discolouration (blueness) at site of injury; limbs/joints can be deformed or oddly shaped; pieces of bone may be piercing through skin.

Action: Summon help immediately. Do not attempt to move the injured person.

Epileptic Seizures

Epilepsy is a condition that causes disturbance in brain pattern, resulting in unconsciousness. There is involuntary movement/jerking of limbs. Clients may bite their tongue and have a loss of continence function during a seizure.

Aim: To minimise injury during the seizure.

Check for: Make sure the area is safe; remove obstacles likely to cause injury during the seizure; loosen all clothing; ensure airway is not obstructed.

Action: Summon immediate medical assistance.

Loss of Consciousness

Causes: Fainting; serious injury or illness.

Check for: Awareness/understanding – may be vague with some responses; no response – unconscious; keep airway clean and clear surrounding area.

Action: Summon help immediately.

Burns/scalds

Aim: Must get assistance immediately. Large burns must be treated in hospital.

Causes: Burns are caused by contact with severe heat/naked flames and electrical currents. Scalds are caused by hot liquids and steam.

Check for: Redness/swelling/tenderness/blistering/peeling/rawness/charring of skin; severe pain will mean nerve endings are damaged (full thickness burns) – usually there are full/partial thickness burns in large burn sites; may suffer from shock; no pain.

Action: Remove watches/rings/jewellery. Reassure client. If clothing is on fire: STOP, DROP, WRAP (on ground to quench flames) and ROLL. **Never remove anything stuck in the wound, touch burned areas or cover the burns (especially facial burns).** Allow medical personnel to decide on appropriate action.

Electric Shock

Electrocution occurs when a current of electricity passes through the body.

Aim: To remove casualty from the area of electrical current.

Check for: Level of consciousness; cardiac arrest (electrocution causes cardiac arrest); burns at entry and exit sites of current.

Action: Immediate medical assistance must be summoned. **Never touch casualty until current is switched off – current should be switched off at mains.**

Poisoning

Causes: An ingestion of substances such as chemicals, plants, drugs, fumes or alcohol.

Check for: This depends on what has been taken but the casualty may be unconscious; complain of pain to mouth/lips; have severe abdominal pain. Check for any visible substances/medicines the casualty might have taken; check for level of consciousness; clear airway if it can be done safely, otherwise don't touch.

Action: Summon immediate medical help.

Severe Bleeding

Aim: Stop bleeding immediately.

Causes: Accident/injury e.g. cuts from glass/mirrors/spikes/sharp edges or sharp instruments like knives/razors/scissors.

Check for: Amount of bleeding and whether it's profuse (spurting/flowing/oozing); source of bleeding and its possible causes; level of consciousness – casualty may be suffering from shock and may eventually lose consciousness.

Action: Requires immediate medical attention. Reassure the patient. **Never take glass or any other foreign body from a bleeding wound.**

Note: Wear gloves and always protect yourself when in contact with blood or any other bodily fluids. Wash hands thoroughly pre- and post-procedure. Cover any skin lesions of your own with a waterproof dressing.

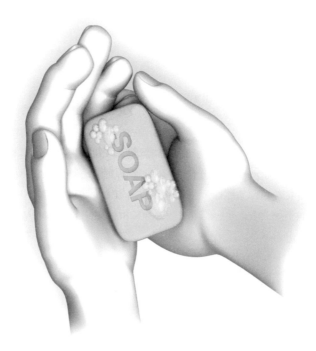

Impact of Living with Chronic Illness

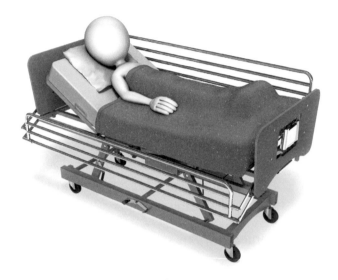

Living with chronic illness is a double-edged sword. There are problems for the client who is chronically ill and there are problems for the family or main carers if the client is in a community setting. As the client loses the ability to make decisions about their care, there are several issues that arise:

- Increasing loss of functions/skills (unable to perform personal tasks)
- Loss of self-esteem/respect/dignity
- Feeling of uselessness
- Dread of having personal tasks done for them
- Fear of complete loss of all skills
- Fear of what will happen eventually (loss of complete independence; unable to make own decisions)
- Fear of pain/suffering
- Fear of death
- Fear of being a burden to family

- Fear of isolation
- Fear of not being understood (as communication lines begins to fail).

Impact on Family and Main Carers

Watching a family member suffer is very difficult. Family members may go through the five stages of loss/bereavement. There are two types of loss within loss itself: sudden loss and loss following chronic illness.

Sudden loss: There is no time to say goodbye, prepare or finalise anything; the wishes are not known. There is a need to adapt coping mechanisms quickly to deal with the situation.

Loss following chronic/long illness: There is more time to adjust to the situation and say goodbye properly as there is more time to go through the stages of grief. The family is able to give time to 'care' for the loved one and find out about the loved one's wishes. Often family arguments can be solved during this time. Physical, emotional, spiritual, social and financial needs can be sorted out during this time.

However, carers may feel anger at:

- Losing a loved one
- Their lack of ability to help them
- The medical profession.

Elder Abuse

Elder abuse is defined as 'a single or repeated act, or lack of appropriate action, occurring within any relationship where there is an expectation of trust, which causes harm or distress to an older person or violates their human and civil rights' (World Health Organization 2002).

The National Centre for the Protection of Older People (2010) records the following types of abuse:

- *Physical abuse:* One or more incidents of physical abuse (e.g. slapped, pushed or physically restrained).

- *Psychological abuse:* Ten or more incidents of psychological abuse (e.g. insulted, threatened or excluded) or any incident that had a serious impact on the older person.

- *Financial abuse:* One or more incidents of financial abuse (e.g. stolen money or possessions, or forced to sign over property).

- *Sexual abuse:* One or more incidents of sexual abuse (e.g. talked to or touched in a sexual way).

- *Neglect:* Ten or more incidents of neglect (e.g. refusal or failure of carer to help with activities of daily living, such as shopping, washing or dressing), or any incident that had a serious impact on the older person.

Demographic Characteristics of People who Reported Mistreatment

In a study carried out in 2010 by the National Centre for the Protection of Older People, it was discovered that women (2.4 per cent) were more likely than men (1.9 per cent) to report experiences of mistreatment in the previous 12 months, in particular financial and interpersonal abuse. People aged 70–79 years and aged 80 years or older experienced similar levels of overall mistreatment; double that of people aged 65–69 years. Those aged 70–79 years experienced more interpersonal abuse, while financial abuse was more common in the other two age groups. Financial abuse increased for both men and women in the 80 years and older age group.

Common Conditions in the Older Person

Chronic Obstructive Airways Disease

Chronic obstructive airways disease (COAD) is a complex disease affecting the lungs. It was ranked as the sixth leading cause of death worldwide in 1990. The two most common conditions of the disease are bronchitis and emphysema.

Bronchitis: This is an inflammation of the bronchi or medium-sized airways. Chronic bronchitis is indicated by an expectorating cough that produces sputum, shortness of breath (dyspnoea) and wheezing.

Emphysema: This causes the destruction of small air sacs called alveoli, resulting in obstruction of the airways, shortness of breath and possible cyanosis (a blue/purple tinge to the skin, mostly noticeable around the lips).

Smoking is the most common cause of both conditions. Adequate respiration is essential to life because all body organs and tissues need oxygen. When there is less oxygen circulating around the blood, the person becomes breathless and cyanosed. The respiratory system shows less age-related decline than any other system in the body of a healthy, non-smoking adult. Older smokers suffer more pronounced consequences because the ill effects of smoking are cumulative.

Stroke

A stroke, also known as cerebrovascular accident (CVA), is caused by the interruption of blood flow to part of the brain, which can be life threatening.

The causes of stroke include:

- Atherosclerosis which narrows and gradually blocks the lumen of the blood vessels to part of the brain. (Atherosclerosis is a disease of the arteries characterised by the deposits of plaques of fatty material on its inner walls.)

- A clot in the blood vessel in the brain which blocks the blood supply.

- A rupture of an artery to part of the brain.

- An embolism which is the part of the clot that breaks off and lodges in a blood vessel in the brain. The affected area of the brain is left without blood supply, therefore without oxygen the person will die.

- A stroke which may occur because blood pressure is too high; this might manifest itself by a history of headaches, dizziness and nose bleeds in the days beforehand.

A stroke can occur suddenly and without warning. The symptoms will depend on the area of the brain involved and the amount of damage to the area. There are areas of the brain that control speech, thinking and movement, and a stroke in the speech area will affect the ability to speak; in the movement area the ability to move. If it occurs in the speech area, it may cause confusion or trouble speaking or understanding speech (dysphasia).

A stroke in one side of the brain will affect the opposite side of the body. Problems such as difficulties with mobility, communication, swallowing and elimination are common following a stroke. The client who has suffered a stroke will require assistance with all the activities of daily living.

Symptoms of stroke include: (*a*) sudden numbness and weakness, especially on one side of the body (hemiplegia); (*b*) difficulty in walking, dizziness or loss of balance or co-ordination; (*c*) sudden trouble seeing in one or both eyes; and (*d*) sudden or severe headaches with no known cause.

The role of the healthcare assistant in caring for the client who has suffered a stroke:

1. Follow the care setting's plan of care.

2. Encourage activity and self-care. Assist with hygiene if needed.

3. Provide a calm environment.

4. Allow time for activities and do not rush the client. Feed the client on the unaffected side.

5. When dressing the client, put clothes on the affected side first and remove clothes from the unaffected side first.

6. Position the client in the correct body alignment and provide support and pressure-relieving devices for affected limbs (e.g. bed and chair).

7. Promote a range of motion exercises as prescribed by the physiotherapist.

8. Encourage the client to use rehabilitation training in daily activities.

9. Provide assistive equipment as needed, e.g. at meal times, such as non-slip mats and plate guards, to encourage independence.

10. Provide mobility aids, such as walking frames.

11. Follow guidelines for communicating with clients with sensory impairment.

12. Observe non-verbal communication.

13. Have patience and empathy.

14. Observe and report any changes in condition.

Arthritis

There are two types of arthritis: osteoarthritis and rheumatoid arthritis.

Osteoarthritis

Most people will have some signs of osteoarthritis when they reach old age as it is the result of wear and tear over the years. Overuse of or trauma to the joints in earlier life will increase the likelihood of it developing.

The condition is caused by the deterioration of the layer of cartilage that covers the end of the bones at a joint. When the cartilage wears down, there is friction between the surfaces of the bone in the joint, causing creaking, grinding and eventually pain. Aches and pain are the most commonly reported symptoms. The pain may start soon after the activity begins and may last for hours after the activity has ceased.

About 50 per cent of sufferers report rest pain and 30 per cent report pain at night. Sensations of tenderness around the affected joint often accompany the pain in the area and may become extremely painful if knocked or handled roughly. Most people also report stiffness. This can mean difficulty in movement, limitation of available range, pain or aching while moving.

The difficulty to get going after rest can initially be severe but sometimes this will only last a few minutes – this is more noticeable in the morning. Weight bearing joints, such as hips, knees, ankles, the joints in the feet and the shoulder joint (from carrying), tend to be affected more.

With the onset of pain the person tends to protect the joint and use it less. This weakens the surrounding muscles making them less able to support the joint. People with osteoarthritis of the knees often describe a feeling of insecurity or instability; a feeling that the joint is going to 'give way'. There is no cure for osteoarthritis but the symptoms can be relieved by anti-inflammatory drugs; pain-killing drugs; joint replacement; physiotherapy, exercise and walking; keeping a normal weight; and specialised aids and equipment.

Rheumatoid arthritis

Rheumatoid arthritis tends to affect the smaller joints such as those in the hands, fingers, wrists and elbows. It can start in early life as a child but is more common in late adulthood. Rheumatoid arthritis is an auto-immune disease, where the immune system reacts against the cells in the synovial membrane, leading to disease by generating local inflammation and tissue damage.

Initial signs include joint inflammation, tenderness of joints and hands, and swelling of joints and hands. Tenderness and swelling can extend to the joints in the wrists and elbows. The person can feel generally unwell as it affects the person's body as a whole and not just the joints.

Symptoms of rheumatoid arthritis include: (*a*) a general feeling of ill health and possible weight loss; (*b*) painful and stiff joints, usually starting in hands and feet; (*c*) swelling of the finger joints, which become stiff, hot and painful; (*d*) joints that will eventually become deformed following muscle wastage; and (*e*) painful contractures, joint instability and deformity which can severely impair mobility.

Careful positioning at night to reduce pain and ward off contractures, as well as discouraging clients from staying too long in the one position during the day, are often elements of caring for this type of person. One of the main symptoms is joint stiffness and this may be alleviated by exercise devised by physiotherapists, which may be done at any time except during an active stage of the condition.

The disease varies in severity with some people affected only slightly while others are badly disabled. As the disease worsens painkillers and anti-inflammatory drugs would be prescribed. People should be encouraged to stay as active as possible to prevent loss of function.

Individual Needs of the Dying Older Person and their Family

Death is a part of life and so it is important that the person dies with dignity and respect in an environment where all needs – physical, emotional, psychological, social and spiritual – are identified and met. Each death is an individual experience unique to the dying person.

People who know that they are dying need to be allowed to make choices about all their care needs. All care plans should have input from the client and family members. They need to be given time and space to grieve for the life they are about to give up.

The dying older person will grieve for the fact that they won't see their grandchildren grow up or their own children's life achievements. They will probably feel very isolated and frightened of the unknown – for dying is a process/journey that everyone must make alone.

The Kubler-Ross Model (1970) identifies the five stages of grief that the dying person may experience:

1. *Denial or isolation:* The person often won't believe the diagnosis/fate.

2. *Anger:* The person thinks 'Why me' and feels angry at the loss of everything.

3. *Bargaining:* The promise to be good/do anything if they can live; known as 'buying time'.

4. *Depression:* The person needs to grieve and come to terms with the inevitable.

5. *Acceptance:* The last stage is a state of calmness/serenity.

Those stages are a defence mechanism against the oncoming unknown – death. The dying person and the family will go through similar stages of grief. Healthcare assistants need to help the client and family to cope with the circumstances surrounding death. Being with someone who is about to die can be physically and emotionally demanding. It is not easy to generalise because of the uniqueness of each individual death, but there are certain factors/strands that are common to individuals/families.

The healthcare assistant's main concern is that the person dies with dignity, and is as comfortable and pain-free as possible. Healthcare assistants need to be trained and educated in the dying process. There are certain aspects of nursing care and carer assistance that need to be addressed:

Pain: Nowadays there is a variety of very effective pain relief available so there is no need for physical discomfort. Pain relief shouldn't need to be requested, it should be anticipated by the nurse.

Skin integrity: Pressure-relieving mattresses can help prevent pressure sores. Barrier creams and physical turning are also highly effective. Close attention needs to be paid to pressure areas while a patient is dying as their skin is especially prone to breakdown.

Indigestion: This can be relieved by antacids.

Nausea/vomiting: These can be relieved by antiemetic drugs.

Diarrhoea/constipation: These can be treated with the use of medication.

Breathing problems: This can be addressed by the upright positioning of a patient, the use of oxygen therapy and appropriate medication as prescribed for individual problems.

Difficulty swallowing: General deterioration or illnesses, such as stroke and dementia, can cause difficulty swallowing. The gag reflex becomes less efficient – the gag reflex is the reflex in the body that ensures food goes down into the oesophagus instead of the respiratory tract (into lungs) when we swallow. When this reflex deteriorates, food or drinks can go down into the lungs, and this is known as aspiration. When aspiration occurs, the client may cough, go pale, become breathless or in some cases have no symptoms.

When a client has no symptoms, it is known as 'silent aspiration'. It is frightening for both the healthcare assistant and the client when aspiration occurs. In order to prevent aspiration, the client should be fed and given drinks only when they are in an upright position. They should never be fed when they are drowsy. If aspiration is feared while feeding a patient, contact a nurse. **Never continue feeding.** If in doubt, get the nurse to check for consciousness/co-operation before commencing feeding.

Aspects of Nursing Care

Aspects of nursing care for the dying older person are the same as for any sick person, for example washing, shaving, bathing, dressing, continence management, mouth care and regular changes of position to prevent pressure sores. They also include:

Communication: Clients need to be spoken to, even if they show no sign of understanding. They need to be reassured and comforted, and made to feel important and dignified.

Emotional support: If the client is conscious, they may need to express fears about their impending death. Ensure questions are answered honestly. Healthcare assistants need to show patience and understanding; they need to learn to be a good listener. Holding the dying person's hand can offer reassurance and comfort – this can be done by carers and family or friends.

Spiritual needs: The client may ask for a minister of religion in whatever denomination is practised. Some religions have rights and practices around death. Healthcare assistants and nurses must observe/record these rites and do whatever they can to facilitate the client's religious or spiritual practices.

Dealing with Fear in the Dying Older Person and their Family

A dying person will have many different fears. These may include fear of:

- Loss of independence
- Loss of self-esteem
- Loss of bladder/bowel control
- Dying alone
- The unknown
- Death itself.

These fears can be alleviated by preparation, a nursing care plan and observation of non-verbal communication.

Families will have the same fears for their loves ones. It is very difficult knowing that a mother or father who was very independent would hate to lose their independence, self-esteem, confidence or basic skills. Healthcare assistants can help the family of the bereaved in a number of ways:

- Allowing the family to talk.

- Allowing the family to express fear.

- Assisting with any physical needs, if the family so desires.

- Giving the family somewhere to rest/talk privately.

- Making refreshments.

- Accommodating phone calls.

- Giving spiritual help, where needed.

- Allowing the family time to speak to the doctor so that they are always up to date with what's happening to their loved one.

- Allowing the family to mourn after the death.

- Allowing the family to spend time with the deceased.

Dying Person's Bill of Rights

I have the right to be treated as a living human being until I die.

I have the right to maintain a sense of hopefulness, however changing its focus may be.

I have the right to be cared for by those who can maintain a sense of hopefulness, however changing this might be.

I have the right to express my emotions and feelings about my approaching death in my own way.

I have the right to participate in decisions concerning my care.

I have the right to expect continuing medical and nursing attention even though cure goals must be changed to comfort goals.

I have the right to die alone.

I have the right to be free of pain.

I have the right to have my questions answered honestly.

I have the right not to be deceived.

I have the right to have help from and for my family in accepting my death.

I have the right to die in peace and dignity.

I have the right to retain my individuality and not be judged for my decisions which may be contrary to the beliefs of others.

I have the right to discuss and enlarge my religious and/or spiritual experience, regardless of what this may mean to others.

I have the right to expect that the sanctity of the human body will be respected after death.

I have the right to be cared for by caring, sensitive and knowledgeable people who will attempt to understand my needs and will be able to gain some satisfaction in helping me face my death.

Respectfully Carrying out Duties after Death

The deceased person's body needs to be treated with the same level of respect as it was treated when the person was alive. Once breathing has stopped, the nurse will check for signs of life before calling a GP to come and check that death has occurred. The nurse checks the following:

- Breathing (stops)

- Heartbeat/pulse (stops after a few beats)

- Level of consciousness (observing if the pupils are fixed and there is no reaction after death has occurred)

- Muscle tone (flaccid/floppy)

- Response to stimuli (none).

The body remains the nurse's/healthcare assistant's responsibility until the body leaves the unit.

Duties after Death

- Note time of death.

- Close eyelids.

- Disconnect any tubing (nasogastric/catheters/IV tubing etc.).

- Put teeth in.

- Replace dressings with clean ones.

- Change any soiled clothes/bed clothes.

- Place hands by sides.

- Cover loosely with clean sheet.

- Close door for privacy.

- Call minister of religion (if one is not already there).

- Leave the body for one hour.

- Allow family to stay with the deceased; try to assist in any practical way that is possible.

- Duties should be carried out quietly, efficiently and with utmost respect for the body.

- Once the body has been pronounced dead by a GP, the family can contact the undertaker.

Nowadays bodies are usually laid out in the mortuary. If this doesn't happen, the body should be washed and dressed in pre-selected clothing and wrapped in a sheet. If death occurs in a nursing home/hospital, the body is usually tagged with the name for identification purposes. All procedure is to be carried out according to hospital/company policies.

Revision Questions

1. What is 'cognition'?

2. List six activities that a client with cognitive impairment may enjoy doing.

3. List six things that healthcare assistants should do when caring for a client with sight impairment.

4. When communicating with a client with a hearing impairment, the healthcare assistant should _____.

5. List five types of mental illnesses.

6. What is 'dementia'?

7. Explain the two main types of dementia.

8. List eight symptoms of dementia.

9. What should the healthcare assistant do in the event of a choking episode?

10. List six effects of chronic illness on a client.

11. List the five stages of grieving.

12. List seven aspects of care that should be addressed in the dying older person.

13. What is 'aspiration'?

14. How can aspiration be prevented?

15. List five fears that the dying older person may have.

Chapter 4

Care Settings

Chapter Outline

- Care settings for the older person
- Quality assurance

Care Settings for the Older Person

Care settings are environments where vulnerable adults and adults with care needs are looked after. Generally, everyone wants to stay in their own familiar environment where they feel safe and where their friends and family are. It is a huge upheaval – physically, emotionally, socially and spiritually – to be uprooted from this environment and put into another; how ever good that new environment might be. One of the most common causes of temporary confusion for older people is being taken from their own surroundings; this is especially so if a confusion or an early dementia is combined with a change in care environment.

Vulnerable adults can be cared for at home with an individually-designed community care programme. These services are usually co-ordinated by a community nurse:

- Community nurse to wash/dress the older person in the morning.

- Home help to do some light housework, shopping etc.

- Carer to put the older person to bed and give a bath/shower as required.

- District nurse gives advice and moral support.

- Emergency call system.

- Input from aids department: bath/shower chair, walking aids e.g. sticks and zimmers.

Care Settings for Older Clients

Members of the Healthcare Team in Each Care Setting

General Hospitals

- Doctors
- Nurses
- Healthcare assistants/carers
- Dentists
- Physiotherapists
- Psychiatrists
- Speech therapists
- Opticians
- Psychologists
- Social workers
- Chiropodists

Residential Homes

- Healthcare assistants/carers
- GPs (visiting)
- Chiropodists
- Hobby therapists
- Social workers
- Practice nurses
- Opticians

Psychiatric Hospitals

- Psychiatrists
- Psychiatric nurses
- Healthcare assistants/carers

- Social workers
- Dentists (visiting)
- GPs (visiting)
- Physiotherapists
- Opticians

Nursing Homes/Residential Facilities

- Nurses
- Healthcare assistants/carers
- GPs (visiting)
- Psychiatrists (visiting)
- Health personnel/district nurses (visiting)
- Practice nurses (visiting)
- Continence nurses (visiting)
- Palliative care staff (visiting)
- Hobby/occupational therapists (visiting)
- Speech therapists (visiting)
- Physiotherapists (visiting)
- Opticians (visiting)

Community Day Centres

- Nurses
- Healthcare assistants/carers
- Practice nurses
- Chiropodists (visiting)
- Social workers (visiting)
- Dentists (visiting)

Home Settings

- Overseen by community nurse
- Community care package
- Home adaptations
- Home help
- Carers from agencies
- Meals on Wheels
- Community carers/nurses
- Palliative care staff
- GPs
- Practice nurses
- Dentists
- Opticians

Retirement Villages

- Wardens

Hospices

- Palliative care staff – nurses/healthcare assistants/carers
- GPs (visiting)
- Social workers (visiting)

Support for the Older Person

- Health professionals
- General practitioner
- Public health nurse
- Occupational therapist

- Physiotherapist
- Voluntary bodies – Meals on Wheels (often operated by friends of a society, community volunteers etc.)
- Day care centres
- Respite care
- Nursing homes

Available Social Services for the Older Person

1. Education
2. Retirement/leaving the workplace
3. Leisure

Education

There are lots of education opportunities for the older person to avail of both locally and nationally. Nowadays older people can study alongside young people, in order to avail of qualifications which they had no opportunity of getting when their children were growing up. There are places available for older people on almost every course, both in further and in higher education. Universities welcome older people. Distance learning opportunities exist for those who want to get an award but cannot devote much time to it. Learning new skills offers the opportunity for an enjoyable social experience as well as the pleasure involved in learning.

Retirement/Leaving the Workplace

Retirement should be planned for in advance, as there are many services and issues to consider:

- Saving and finances

- Pension provision

- Housing (living conditions; situation of house)

- Dietary needs

- Medical expenses (if not without charge)

- Transport (personal use)

- Availability and proximity of services (church, shops, social centre, transport, family or other supportive networks)

- What services are available free of charge? (Get 'Entitlements for Over Sixties')

- Keeping in touch with work colleagues, friends and family.

Retirement is a time to 'wind down' and disengage. People believe that retirement marks a transition to old age – the shedding of pressure-filled work roles and the onset of more restful and enjoyable pursuits/lifestyles.

There are different attitudes towards leaving the workplace which depend, of course, on outlook, adequate or inadequate preparation, whether one is alone or still has a partner, adequate medical provision, how fit and healthy one may be, and personal interests. If the retired person has a good social circle that continues into retirement, it can contribute to overall wellbeing. Lack of preparation or not examining options may lead to boredom/lack of direction. Often husbands and wives get under each other's feet. They need to have personal pursuits as well as interests they can share together.

When given a choice, most people want to retire as soon as they can afford to. They can't wait to leave the workforce and are looking forward to being able to do things in a leisurely manner, and to have plenty of time to explore pursuits and visit family. Often, the reality is that they miss the camaraderie of the workplace, and are lonely and without focus. They certainly have more leisure time but maybe they don't have the resources (if living on a pension) to do what they would like.

Ralmore *et al.* (1985) describe how older adults who adjust to retirement best are healthy, active and well educated; they have adequate incomes, extended social networks, including both family and friends, and were usually satisfied with their lives pre-retirement. Stull and Hatch (1984) state that older adults with inadequate incomes, poor health and other stresses which occur, for example retirement, death of spouse or health concerns, have the most difficult time adjusting to retirement.

Leisure

Leisure time is very important. If people work well and work hard, it is important that they have some free time to relax and do something that is stress-free. The classical view of leisure is that it is a state of mind. Leisure may depend on social class. If we examine the pursuit of leisure during the past, people had very little opportunity or were too tired to have any leisure pursuits because of the length of the working day (in some cases the average week was 72 hours). At that point in history only the elite could pursue leisure activities while the working class were condemned to a life of constant work. Nowadays we can work part-time or flexi-time to suit a certain lifestyle or home life, or we can work long days so that contact time at work is reduced.

Leisure pursuits can include any activity that has a therapeutic effect, such as the following:

- Watching television (sports, current affairs, the news, historical programmes, educational programmes, films etc.)
- Reading, writing and doing crosswords
- Cinema visits
- Arts and crafts (making things, creating things, learning new crafts e.g. crochet, picture making, painting, interior design, flower arranging and cookery)
- Cards (poker, bridge etc.)
- Games (bingo, board games etc.)
- Walking
- Swimming
- Physical activities (gym activities, playing golf etc.)
- Gardening
- Travel and camping
- Outings (driving for pleasure)
- Dining out
- Weekends away
- Hill climbing
- Organisations/clubs (providing entertainment, music, dancing in the company of friends, quiz evenings etc.)
- Attending/producing plays and musicals

- Library facilities
- Coffee mornings
- Tea dances.

Quality Assurance

Standards

A set of standards is a basis for assessment and provides definitions for what is required. Therefore, a set of standards is a system for defining outcomes: defining what needs to be achieved and giving guidelines on what needs to be done to achieve the required outcomes. It defines areas of skill, value and knowledge, and targets which need to be achieved, so that the required standards are upheld. Standards can be national, local or in-house. Good standards are important for good care delivery.

In order for standards to be set and maintained, it is important that staff are trained in the care of older people. There are moral and ethical considerations for any services that are provided, such as distribution of services, advocacy, ageism and consent for treatment. Normally these are in the domain of professional associations which decide through guidelines and legislation what they consider to be best practice.

Once standards are set, they need to be monitored and updated periodically. This usually requires a governing body to test and measure performances on an on-going basis; then to award the standard when required targets are met.

Quality

In 1994 the National Health Strategy defined quality as a key component in the delivery of all healthcare provision. For older people the most important aspects are *quality of life* and *quality of care*.

Quality of Life

Quality of life defines how people feel about what happens in their life. In order to promote quality of life, the older person must be assisted to remain autonomous and to have their dignity preserved. For this to happen, all care deliverers should develop and monitor standards.

Care deliverers can include medical and nursing staff, homecare managers, and family and friends of the older person. Older people should, as far as possible, be involved in all decisions regarding their own care. The ideal situation is for standards to be uniform and measurement indicators/goals similar.

Quality of Care

Quality of care is concerned with the type of care being delivered. Individual care plans are formulated so that each client has a plan designed from the 12 Activities of Daily Living, which is unique to their specific needs. Care plans are long term and/or short term. They are reviewed on a three-monthly basis unless there is a change in circumstances for the client, in which case a new plan is designed. The care plan used by most hospitals/nursing homes is the Roper, Logan & Tierney Model of Nursing.

For a quality service to be successful, written standards and outcomes need to be in place. In Irish healthcare, performance measurement is in its infancy and will require investment of time and money to ensure success; a national strategy needs to be developed by all interested parties with relevant performance indicators and achievable goals. Most care deliverers have their own set of policies and procedures, and those policies would all be roughly similar. Standards in nursing homes are monitored by the Health Information Quality Authority, Health Act 2007 and National Quality Standards for Residential Care Settings for Older People 2009.

Health Information and Quality Authority

The Health Information and Quality Authority (HIQA) was developed as a result of the Health Act 2007. It is an independent authority which has been established to drive continuous improvement in Ireland's healthcare and social care services, and was established as part of the Government's overall Health Service Reform Programme.

HIQA's mandate extends across the public, private (within its social care function) and voluntary sectors in the promotion of quality and safety in the provision of health and personal social services. HIQA reports directly to the Minister for Health and Children.

HIQA has statutory responsibility for:

- *Setting standards for health and social services:* Developing person-centred standards, which are based on evidence and best international practice, for health and social care services in Ireland (except mental health services).

- *Monitoring healthcare quality:* Monitoring standards of quality and safety in the health services; implementing continuous quality assurance programmes to promote improvements; and, as deemed necessary, undertaking investigations into suspected and serious service failure in healthcare.

- *Health technology assessments:* Ensuring the best outcome for the service user by evaluating the clinical and economic effectiveness of drugs, equipment, diagnostic techniques and health promotion activities.

- *Health information:* Advising on the collection and sharing of information across the services; and evaluating and publishing information about the delivery and performance of Ireland's health and social care services.

- *The Social Services Inspectorate:* Responsible for the registration and inspection of residential homes for children, older people and people with disabilities; monitoring day- and pre-school facilities and children's detention centres; and inspecting foster care services.

HIQA's approach to the development of standards for health and social care services is informed by the following key principles:

- *Openness and transparency:* To ensure that the general public is informed of the development of standards and the decision-making process.

- *Focus on outcomes:* To ensure that the implementation of standards will result in meaningful, tangible and real improvements in services.

- *Person-centredness:* To ensure that all stakeholders, including service users and those who deliver health and social services, are involved in the development of standards.

- *Evidence-based practice:* To ensure that the standards are underpinned by up-to-date, peer reviewed national and international research.

The National Quality Standards for Residential Care Settings for Older People were developed by HIQA in 2009. They set out the quality and safety standards of the service for an older person living in a residential care setting. For service providers these standards provide a road map of continuous improvement to support the on-going development and provision of person-centred, accountable care. HIQA inspectors have the authority to visit a nursing home announced or unannounced.

TASK

Discuss the HIQA standards and their implications for your role.

HIQA inspectors include members from the following departments:

1. Medical department

2. Environmental health department

3. Occupational health department.

1. *Medical department:* This consists of a doctor and a nurse, who check nursing standards (by examining the care plan); staffing levels (in conjunction with dependency rating scales); and staff training files (to check job-specific training). There are three statutory trainings: moving and handling; fire; and the Control of Substances Hazardous to Health (COSHH). They also check:

- Medicine administration.

- Customer satisfaction by talking to clients/relatives, getting opinion and checking if there are complaints.

- Accident books and ensure that risk assessment on accidents are up to date.

- Day-to-day records (one report for daytime and one for night).

- Administration and discharge records.

- Policies and procedures (the care setting must have a system for up-to-date review).

- The planned activity programme, which nursing homes have an obligation to provide (the programmes must be client- and age-orientated and the level of activities suitable for existing clientele in the care settings).

- All equipment – bells, buzzers etc.

2. *Environmental Health Department:* This department monitors standards and checks anything to do with the ordering, delivery, storage, cooking, cooling and reheating of food, as well as the disposal of food waste. They ensure that all kitchen staff (chefs and kitchen assistants) have relevant, up-to-date training (to national requirement). They ensure that all kitchens have a hazard analysis critical control point (HACCP) system in place. Water is checked for contamination by e-coli etc.

Overall, the nursing home is checked to ensure that it is a clean and safe environment. The department usually visits bi-annually but can come to do a check at any time.

3. *Occupational Health Department:* This department checks that the design of the building is appropriate; size of rooms conform to plan; hand rails, including shower and toilet rails, are at the correct height; toilet seats for disability toilets are higher than standard size; and equipment is in working order, changed and ready for use (hoists, wheelchairs, bathing chairs etc.).

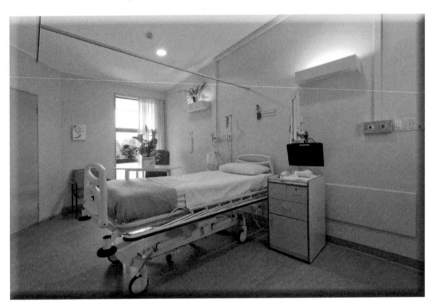

Revision Questions

1. List some of the effects relocation (moving from home to a nursing home/hospital) has on clients.

2. List some things that may be included in community care programmes/packages.

3. Name some of the educational opportunities that exist for older adults.

4. What is 'retirement'?

5. How can people prepare for retirement?

6. What is an example of a 'standard' as laid out by HIQA?

7. How can standards be set out and maintained?

8. What is meant by 'quality'?

9. How can 'quality of life' be maintained?

10. How can 'quality of care' be achieved?

11. What three departments make up the registration team that monitors standards in nursing homes?

Final Questions

Keep these questions for assessment reference.

1. What is the role of the healthcare assistant?

2. What support and benefits are available to the healthcare assistant?

Abbreviations Used in Healthcare

An abbreviation is a shortened form of a word. Abbreviations can save time and space when writing to communicate. It is very important that only approved abbreviations are used. Each hospital or care setting should have a list of approved abbreviations and it is the responsibility of the healthcare worker to find out what ones are approved for use, as not all hospitals/care settings use the same abbreviations.

Using approved abbreviations allows all staff to understand what is meant and it prevents mistakes being made. It can be dangerous to use unapproved abbreviations as many interpretations can be assumed to be right and the consequences can be extremely dangerous for the client. If there is uncertainty surrounding the meaning of an abbreviation, the word should be written in full to prevent it being interpreted incorrectly. (See lists of some approved abbreviations and medical terminology below. **Note:** It is essential to check in your place of work for the approved list.)

Terminology Used in Nursing

An acronym is the name given to abbreviations where the first letters of the words are used, for example RGN for Registered General Nurse. As a rule, the word should be written in full the first time it is used and the acronym follows in brackets, for example Attention Deficit Disorder (ADD); then the acronym is used each subsequent time. The use of acronyms on nursing reports or medical documents can be dangerously misleading because some acronyms have several different meanings.

Examples of Approved Abbreviations and Medical Terminology	
ADD	Attention Deficit Disorder
ADHD	Attention Deficit Hyperactivity Disorder
ADLs	Activities of Daily Living
AIDS	Acquired Immune Deficiency Syndrome
Am	Morning
BP	Blood Pressure
C&S	Culture and Sensitivity
CHD	Coronary Heart Disease
COPD	Chronic Obstructive Pulmonary Disease
CPR	Cardiopulmonary Resuscitation
CSU	Catheter Specimen of Urine
CVA	Cerebrovascular Accident (stroke)
Dementia	Death or malfunction of brain cells, causing confusion and eventual inability to carry out ADLs
DOB	Date of Birth
Enuresis	Bedwetting, usually refers to children
FOB	Faecal Occult Blood
GI	Gastro Intestinal
Glaucoma	High pressure in the eyeball leading to blindness
H_2O	Water
Hb	Haemoglobin (red blood cell count)
Hep A, B or C	Hepatitis
HIV	Human Immunodeficiency Virus
Hr	Hour
Hyper	Raised
Hypo	Lowered
Hyperglycaemia	High blood sugar levels

Hypoglycaemia	Low blood sugar levels
Hypertension	High blood pressure
Hypotension	Low blood pressure
I&O	Intake and Output
ICU	Intensive Care Unit
Incontinence	Reduced or loss of bowel or bladder control in adults
LMP	Last Menstrual Period
MSU	Midstream Specimen of Urine
N/G Tube	Naso-gastric tube
NPO	Nil by mouth
O_2	Oxygen
Osteoporosis	Loss of bone density, leading to breakages
OT	Occupational Therapy
PEG tube	Percutaneous Endoscopy Gastrostomy Tube
PO	By mouth
Postop	Postoperatively (after surgery)
Preop	Preoperatively (before surgery)
Prep	Preparation
PRN	When necessary/as required
MS	Multiple Sclerosis
TEDs	Thrombo Embolic Deterrent Stockings
TPR	Temperature, Pulse and Respiration
UTI	Urinary Tract Infection
Wt	Weight

Prescriptive Medical Terminology	
1 mane	Take one tablet in the morning
1 bd	One tablet twice daily, usually morning and evening
I tid	One tablet three times daily, usually morning, midday & evening
1 qid	One tablet four times daily, usually morning, midday, evening and night
1 nocte	One at night, usually at bedtime
An emetic	A substance to induce vomiting
IMI	Intramuscular injection
IVI	Intravenous injection
Subcut	Subcutaneous (under the skin and refers to injections e.g. diabetic insulin is given subcut)

Abbreviations and Terms for Health Disciplines	
APN	Advanced Practice Nurse
CNS	Clinical Nurse Specialist
CPN	Community Psychiatric Nurse
CWO	Community Welfare Officer
GP	General Practitioner
NT	Nurse Tutor
OT	Occupational Therapist
PHN	Public Health Nurse
Physio	Physiotherapist
RCN	Registered Children's Nurse
RM	Registered Midwife
RN	Registered Nurse
RPsN	Registered Psychiatric Nurse
SLT	Speech and Language Therapist

Guide to Falls Prevention in the Home

The problems associated with a fall increase as the person gets older. This guide is designed to help the older person, their relatives and their carer minimise the risk of falling. By encouraging the older person to follow a few simple steps, the possibility of danger can be reduced and it can make the home a safer place.

1. Encourage regular exercise, even if it is only a short walk, to keep muscles strong and joints supple.

2. Easy-grip handrails should be fitted on both sides of the stairs. Climbing stairs should be avoided/minimised if the older person does not feel safe climbing them.

3. Stairs and living areas should be well lit (100 watt bulbs are recommended) and a torch and a phone should be kept by the bed.

4. Objects should never be left on stairs or in walking areas. Flexes and cables should not cross walking areas. Worn rugs and carpets should be replaced and the edges of rugs can be nailed or taped down to avoid slips and trips.

5. Non-slip rubber mats can be used in the bath or shower and a handrail fitted near the bath and toilet. Avoid small rugs in the bathroom.

6. If prescribed medication is making the older person feel dizzy, advise them to consult a GP as soon as possible.

7. Rock salt should be kept handy to put on external paths in cold weather.

8. To minimise bending and climbing, frequently used items can be kept on racks or in drawers at an easy-to-reach level. Have a letter tray and a rack for milk deliveries fitted.

9. If climbing must be done, advise the use of proper steps and never chairs or tables, which may be unstable.

10. Encourage slow movement when getting up from chairs and bed. Blood pressure falls as a person rises and the body may take longer to adjust as it gets older.

11. Advise against poor-fitting shoes, slippers and high heels. A good walking shoe is recommended in and out of the home.

12. Encourage regular eye tests. It is possible in many areas now to have an eye test at home. Bifocals should not be worn on the stairs.

13. Clothes that may cause trips should be avoided, such as trailing nightdresses.

14. The telephone need not be answered in a rush. Friends can be warned that it may take longer to reach the telephone. Have an extension socket fitted upstairs.

Prevention of falls is essential as many fractures happen due to falls. Falls are linked to osteoporosis; this is why prevention or treatment of osteoporosis is also essential. One in five men and one in two women over 50 will break bones due to osteoporosis. Twenty per cent of people aged 60 and over who fracture their hip will die within 6–12 months and 50 per cent of people aged 60 and over who fracture their hip will not be able to wash, bathe or walk across a room unaided. Ninety per cent of hip fractures are due to osteoporosis but only 15 per cent of people are diagnosed with it.

If a client has the potential to fall, the registered nurse should complete a falls risk assessment. The care setting should have a falls prevention policy also.

Glossary

Health

The World Health Organization describes health as a state of complete physical, mental and social wellbeing, not merely the absence of disease or infirmity.

Physical health covers the normal functioning of the body.

Mental health covers the health of the mind and the ability to think clearly and carry out intellectual processes. It also includes the ability to express emotions and cope with mental demands like stress and worry.

Social health is the ability to form relationships, both personally and professionally. In fact, loneliness can contribute to ill health.

The three aspects (physical, mental and social) are interrelated and each can impact on the other. Therefore, the approach to health is a 'holistic' approach. An individual's state of health can have an effect on everything else they do, for example work, learning, potential and lifestyle. (Moonie 1996)

Healthy Ageing

Healthy ageing is the process by which there is a physical and psychological deterioration of body and mind. Gross motor and fine manipulative skills can be affected by loss of muscle power and bone diseases, for example arthritis whereby walking is slowed down. There are many factors that affect ageing, such as heredity, environment, lifestyle, and physical and mental health. The social impacts of ageing include retirement, lack/loss of income, family leaving home, increasing dependency, bereavement and pain/disease. All the above factors can contribute to the process of ageing 'speeding up'.

Environment

Environment means the surroundings that a person or people function in – everything that can affect people in a physical and social context. This includes air and water quality, landscape, housing and noise.

Genetic

Genetic means relating to or descriptive of an entire group or class.

Demography

Demography means the study of the characteristics of human population, such as size, growth, density, distribution and vital statistics. Demographic data means the collection of information of national or global trends.

Demographic trends are affected by population (the increase and decrease of birth and death rates), disease (the increase and eradication of diseases), emigration, immigration, diminishing labour force, war, disasters (earthquakes, tsunamis, flooding etc.), ageing population, the physically and psychologically challenged etc.

For future planning, health and social planners must consider what kind of care service elderly people will need, what kind of care elderly people will want, the type of staff who will provide these care/education needs and what kind of care government/local services will provide (dependent on economic factors).

Dementia

Dementia is a term that covers a wide range of illnesses involving the degeneration (or wasting) of the brain. Dementia is not a part of normal ageing; most very old people show no sign of this illness.

Concepts

Concepts are ways of thinking which enable people to understand and make more sense of the world. Concepts are also linguistic (language) terms used to classify, predict and explain physical and social reality. They are probably dependent on experience of events and are useful in terms of simplifying experience and for their ability to be shared with others.

Retirement

Retirement can be defined as the end of a working life. The usual retirement age in contracts of employment is 65. Retirement should be planned for and a pre-retirement course recommended. The following key areas should also be addressed: healthcare, financial provision, housing, social needs and leisure provision/social interests.

Status

A measure of the rank and prestige of a person or group of people. Status helps to define how people see themselves and how they are treated by others. Status is linked to role and different roles in a group have various levels of status attached to them.

Social Status

The value a group places on a particular social role, thus giving credibility and respect to that role, for example the leader of a group of teenagers because they can organise others or perhaps control the group through fear; a judge because of the knowledge and power to uphold the laws of society. Social status may be due to money or possessions, but these will vary depending on the culture of the groups within society.

Ethnic

The word ethnic is used to describe people who have a common ancestry, geographical place of origin and cultural tradition. They may share the same language, literature, music, traditions etc. Ethnic traditions are peculiar to a group of people who share a common bond.

Culture

Culture can be described as a collection of ideas and habits shared by a given group i.e. the norms and value base of a group. They help to reinforce the identity of the group, making it different from other groups. Individuals learn the roles acceptable to others within their culture. Cultures have their own system of values, which may be linked to religious beliefs. The culture we are raised in can be one of the biggest influences in our lives.

Values

Learned principles or systems that enable individuals to choose between alternatives and make decisions. Values guide behaviour in relation to what is judged to be 'valuable'. Values are learned in a cultural context and will develop in relation to the beliefs and norms that exist within a cultural group.

Confidentiality

The right of clients to have private information about themselves restricted to people who have an approved need of vital statistics.

Empowerment

Empowerment means giving necessary information and/or equipment/tools that may result in giving 'control' to the client. This helps to maintain client independence and self-esteem; it allows clients to feel important and valued; and it gives clients control over their daily lives and activities, as far as possible.

In order to empower someone, it is important that the healthcare assistant's attitude is non-discriminatory. There must be respect for a client's beliefs and identity, and once decisions have been made about rights and choices, the healthcare assistant must support and uphold those choices. A client knows their own needs best and should be assisted in the identification and implementation of whatever it takes to meet those needs. It is important to maintain effective communication and confidentiality at all times.

Holistic

Holistic comes from the word holism – the theory that reality is made up of organic or unified wholes that are greater than the simple sum of their parts. Holistic means of or pertaining to holism; it emphasises the importance of the whole and the interdependence of its parts.

Cognition

Cognition is a term that refers to the mental processes involved in understanding and knowing.

Self-confidence

An individual's confidence in their own ability to achieve something or cope with a situation.

Stereotype

A way of grouping people, objects or events together and attributing individuals with the same qualities and characteristics. Stereotyping can help the individual to make sense of the world by making predictions easier. Stereotyping may have positive or negative consequences.

Ethics

The moral codes that form the basis of decision making; therefore, the behaviour of workers in a given profession.

Course Information

Here is a list of resources and places to go for information:

- Internet
- Local newspapers
- Libraries — books, newspapers, journals, magazines
- DVDs/videos/radio/TV
- Health centres
- Hospitals
- GP surgeries
- Chemists
- Shops e.g. health food shops
- Community centres
- Businesses
- Department of Health
- Schools
- Teachers
- Supervisors
- Fellow students
- Work colleagues
- Local councils
- Personal experience
- Personal experience of someone you know
- Previous work experience
- Registry offices for statistics and archives
- Charities
- Campaign groups
- Politicians/political parties
- Lessons
- Yellow Pages.

References

Department of Health, *Shaping a Healthier Future: A Strategy for Effective Healthcare in the 1990s* (Dublin: Stationery Office, 1994)

Department of Health and Social Security, *Black Report* (London: Department of Health and Social Security, 1980)

International Labour Organization, *World Employment Report* (Geneva: International Labour Organization, 1995)

Kübler-Ross, E., *On Death and Dying* (London: Tavistock Publications, 1970)

Moonie, N., *Advanced Health and Social Care* (Oxford: Heinemann Educational Publishers, 1996)

Moonie, N. and Aldworth, C., *Core Themes in Health and Social Care* (Oxford: Pearson Education, 2007)

National Centre for the Protection of Older People, *Abuse and Neglect of Older People in Ireland: Report on the National Study of Elder Abuse and Neglect* (Dublin: UCD and HSE, 2010)

Palmore, E. B., *Retirement: Causes and Consequences* (New York: Springer Publishing Company, 1985)

Parnes, H. S., Crowley, J. E., Haurin, R. J., Less, L. J. , Morgan, W. R., Mott, F. L. and Nestal G. (eds), *Retirement among American Men* (Lexington, Massachusetts: Lexington Books, 1986)

Rybash J. M., Roodin P. A. and Hoyer W. J., *Adult Development and Ageing* (New York: McGraw Hill, 2005)

Stull, D. E. and Hatch L. R., 'Unravelling the Effects of Multiple Life Changes', *Research on Aging* 6(4) (1984) 560–571

World Health Organization, *Missing Voices: Views of Older Persons on Elder Abuse* (Geneva: World Health Organization/International Network for the Prevention of Elder Abuse, 2002)